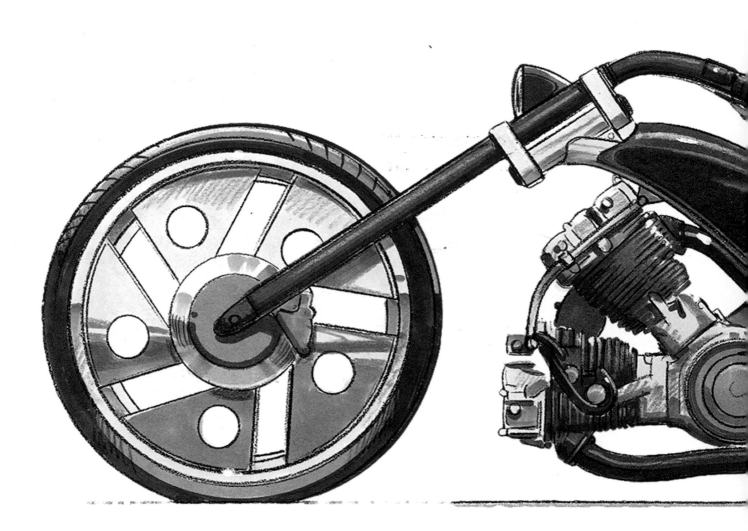

# HOW TO DRAW
# CHOPPERS
## LIKE A PRO

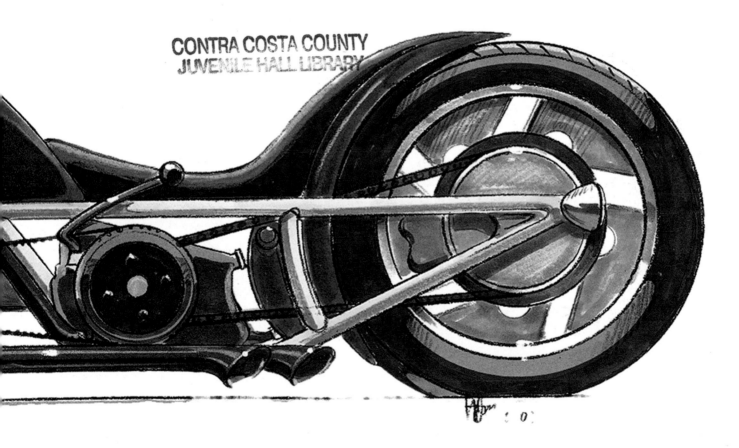

# THOM TAYLOR
## FOREWORD BY ARLEN NESS

**MOTORBOOKS**

First published in 2005 by Motorbooks, an imprint of MBI Publishing Company, Galtier Plaza, Suite 200, 380 Jackson Street, St. Paul, MN 55101-3885 USA

Motorbooks titles are also available at discounts in bulk quantity for industrial or sales-promotional use. For details write to Special Sales Manager at MBI Publishing Company, Galtier Plaza, Suite 200, 380 Jackson Street, St. Paul, MN 55101-3885 USA.

ISBN-13: 978-0-7603-2260-4
ISBN-10: 0-7603-2260-0

Editor: Dennis Pernu
Designer: Kou Lor

Printed in China

**On the frontispiece:** The fun things about a Dave Deal cartoon are the people, as well as how he exaggerates the vehicle. Dave scans his pen or pencil sketches, then colors them in Photoshop.

**On the title page:** Author Thom Taylor illustrates—literally—how to get the most out of few colors and gradation.

**On the back cover:** The author's cover drawing in progress. Whether your interests lie in doodling or designing your dream bike, the principles outlined by Thom Taylor can put you on the road to some exciting illustrations.

**About the author:**
Renowned car designer Thom Taylor is a four-time winner of the coveted "America's Most Beautiful Roadster" award and an inductee into the Hot Rod Hall of Fame. A graduate of Pasadena's Art Center College of Design, Taylor has designed cars for industry-leading builders like Boyd Coddington and Roy Brizio, as well as celebrities Eric Clapton, Tim Allen, and Billy F Gibbons of ZZ Top. In addition to creating signature die-cast lines for Racing Champions, Revell, and Testors, he is the author of the Motorbooks bestseller *How to Draw Cars Like a Pro*. Taylor lives in Southern California.

# Contents

# Acknowledgments

Almost 10 years after I did *How To Draw Cars Like a Pro* with my wife, Lisa, Motorbooks finally got me away from my normal design and art projects to do this book, which I'm thrilled to be able to present to you. As with my other projects, things like writing and compiling a book aren't done alone.

To the artists and designers who have contributed both their time and art, thanks so much. It is the best part for me—being able to include you in something I do—for you are either good friends or artists whom I have admired for years but not had the chance to get to know really well.

Some of the art in this book is not "chopper" art in the strictest sense. For instance, Tom Fritz and Jim Bruni have work that is heavily into the vintage board-track and racing end of the American motorcycle. However, all the chopper guys I know love the vintage stuff and, in some cases, have built modern interpretations of that look. And the racers were modified Harleys and Indians, just like many choppers are today. The bottom line: the artwork is so superior, and the subject matter so cool, how could you not dig it?

Three guys who have nothing to do with two-dimensional art, but have been creating three-dimensional art for years, helped with this book as well. To Arlen Ness, thanks for the foreword, and for the past and future projects we have been or will be involved with. There's one thing about Arlen: when you do a drawing for him, you know it will be built. Also to Bob Dron for sharing some of Don Varner's design sketches. Bob has done many a cool Harley project over the years, and he owns *the* Harley dealership in the country (to my way of seeing things): Harley-Davidson of Oakland, California—the heart of the chopper movement, Hell's Angels, and lots more. And to Ron Simms, owner of Bay Area Customs, for the use of some of my design sketches done eons ago for you.

I especially want to thank the King of Car Cartoons, Dave Deal, for documenting the stages of the cartoon he did exclusively for this book (see Chapter Twelve). I'm honored!

At Motorbooks, thanks to Zack Miller for being editor on the *Cars* book and, though he's moved up in the company, for helping to put this book deal together. Also to my editor on this one, Dennis Pernu, who put up with my long-winded phone conversations, and to Tim Parker.

To my wife, Lisa, and children, James and Chloe, thanks for letting me take the time to churn this one out. I love you all.

Finally, to someone I never met but was hoping to include in this book, the late Dave Mann. He died just a month or two before I started this and was going to be my first call for art and inspiration. He is the person I think of most when it comes to choppers and art. Since the early '70s—first with the 20 or so Ed "Big Daddy" Roth posters, and then in the pages of *Easyriders*—he had presented the biker lifestyle with cool paintings that have stimulated many a budding artist. As Keith Richards once said, "The good ones go young, so what's that say about me?"

So grab for third gear and let's go for an adventure—let's draw some choppers!

# Foreword

When I first started building bikes, I was exploring ways to make my choppers distinctive by changing the length of forks and fenders, altering frames, or even playing around with twin V-twin engines in a single bike. Later on, when I wanted to develop an entire bike with my own ideas instead of merely changing a component or two, drawing became essential to help me figure out the overall look of a bike—right down to the shape of a tank or air foil. Drawing is also a great tool for showing the metal-shaper what I want, so that I got what I want.

In the early 1990s I decided to customize my Ferrari, and I asked Thom to help out with some ideas. Once I was done, I was interested in doing a custom bike that incorporated styling elements from that Ferrari, and so I called on Thom to come up with some drawings for what became my "Big Red" blown custom. Craig Naff was the metal-shaper on that project, and Thom's drawings became an indispensable tool for Craig, instantly showing him what I wanted.

During the building of Big Red, Thom also did some really loose sketches for what became my Indian-inspired "Sled" convertible custom. Again, between my own sketches and Thom's, I was able to nail down what the design would look like, and to convey that to the metal-shaper.

More recently, Carl Brewer has been my designer whenever I get into a bike project that requires the building of a body. With a rough idea, I will build the frame and get the bike rolling, take pictures for Carl to reference, and then go see him to talk over my ideas. He did the drawings for my turbine-motor "Jet Bike," and also the wild "Top Banana" custom I built for one of the recent *Biker Build-Off* television shows. With so many bike builders exploring styling, proportion, and details to distinguish their bikes from the next guy's, designing a bike with some exciting aluminum bodywork is one way to create a really distinctive custom.

My son, Cory, has handled the designing chores for our Harley-Davidson components and accessories product lines for years. He does pencil sketches of what the component will look like and sometimes draws them to scale as well. Once this is done, he takes them to our in-house engineer, Paul Mitchell. Cory and Paul work together on the computer to figure out the structural and stress issues before the design is put on a tape that directs the five-axis mill we use for so many of our exclusive aluminum parts and accessories. So, we here at Arlen Ness utilize drawings every day for one aspect of the business or another.

Thom has been working with many of the top hot rod and chopper builders for over 25 years and has been so valuable to them and their customers. His sketches and designs have inspired all of us, and hopefully that same inspiration will guide you to draw like a pro.

Who knows, if you get really proficient with your drawing and designing skills, I may someday be using you to help me with a future bike neither you nor I have even dreamed of yet!

—*Arlen Ness, March 2005*

▲ Custom-bike and chopper legend Arlen Ness. *Michael Lichter*

# A Quick History of the Chopper

Gangs of drunken bikers, like marauding wolves out of control, rage through one city after another on their deadly, mad motorcycles. Murder, rape, destruction, and worse are all that is left in their bloody path. No child, woman, or man is safe from their wanton, devilish swath of cannibalization. The world is surely doomed by the mere thought of these roving, reckless mobs of gangsters and their menacing, maniacal machines.

Does this sound familiar? Really, isn't this the reputation that bikers and their choppers have realized since coming to the American consciousness just after World War II? Pretty crazy, isn't it? So how did such a cool thing as personalizing, refining, and enjoying these two-wheel wonderments get such a screwed-up reputation? Let's try to piece together a little history of the American chopper.

▶ Lighter, louder, faster. For some postwar riders, performance and handling superseded pure utility. These motorcyclists borrowed a page from hot rodders by stripping their stock bikes of all unnecessary weight, oftentimes removing the fenders entirely or "bobbing" them to leave only the barest amount of sheet metal—thus the term "bobber." Today, builders like Arlin Fatland of Colorado pay homage to this aesthetic. *Michael Lichter*

◄ In 1954, Hollywood fictionalized the infamous 1947 Fourth of July Gypsy Tour and Races in Hollister, California, with *The Wild One*. If the sometimes equally fictionalized press surrounding the original event didn't seal motorcyclists' sullied image with John Q. Public, this outlaw biker epic starring Lee Marvin and Marlon Brando certainly did the trick. *Courtesy Mike Seate Collection*

Before choppers, there were stock bikes with a mission: to transport their rider cheaply, reliably, comfortably, and with a practicality that included features like bags to haul your junk, plex-windshields to keep the bugs out of your teeth, footboards for comfort and protection, and more.

To some, the need for performance and better handling became paramount over picking up groceries or transporting family and friends. Replacing the heavy, restrictive exhaust systems with something lighter and louder, and pitching the heavy bags and comfort features (like those big padded seats, footboards, and windshields)—basically removing as much unneeded weight as possible, even down to primary chain guards, front brakes, and horns—lightened up the bike and instantly made it faster and more agile. Removing the fenders entirely or "bobbing" them to leave only the barest amount of sheet metal protection from mud and gravel not only cut even more weight but looked cool. Thus was begat the term "bobber."

Bobbing could also mean throwing away the rear fender and replacing it with the more abbreviated front fender, turned backward. Whatever the method, these cut-down, lightened-up bobbers were faster, had better handling, and were just plain cooler-looking. So what do you do with a bobber on the street? Show off and go fast, what else? This became the first nail in the coffin for the bad-biker image.

Of course, a lot of these stripped-down bikes were raced in different events. Speed trials were one such venue not unlike hot rodders' "lakes modifieds" at Southern California dry lakes. In many ways, the development of the chopper parallels the development of the hot rod—from its time line, to the reasons for and influences on the modifications performed, to the reputations of the owners and builders involved in these "reckless endeavors." Other venues for motorcycle racing included hill climbs and speedways; the latter could mean asphalt tracks, dirt flat tracks, and in the 1920s, board tracks—actual wooden racetracks elevated and banked for high-speed spectacles. By the end of the 1920s, however, deterioration of the wood and the sheer butchery resulting from a wipeout or crash spelled doom for the board tracks scattered throughout the country. But motorcycle racing continued under the auspices of the American Motorcycle Association (AMA).

With the advent of World War II, the massive war effort halted all manner of sports activities. Young men were shipped off to fight in Europe and Asia, where

some learned the mechanics of tanks, airplanes, and even motorcycles, which would prime their knowledge for the day when they could return to American soil and resume their riding and racing passions.

The fun, coolness, and excitement of flying on a fast motorcycle spread from one GI motorcycle enthusiast to another. That enthusiasm, combined with the natural pent-up energy that existed for anything and everything American when overseas, brought a huge number of servicemen (those lucky enough to survive the war) to many a local motorcycle dealership when the hostilities were over. Once they had their bikes, hanging out with like-minded pals spawned many new regional clubs, which led to a collision of styles, philosophies, and manners between the AMA and this new breed of motorcycle rider.

The AMA was made up of motorcycle clubs that put together races and events for their like-minded brethren before and after the war. Common uniforms and strict manners and codes were the norm. The bikes were conservative and close to stock, if not completely stock. You could compare it to 1950s bowling leagues or Ralph Kramden and his lodge brothers. After the war, the new clubs that sprang up took on a lot of the trappings of their members' lives during wartime—things such as wearing flight jackets and tall leather boots, and even painting on their bikes the nose art that decorated the huge bombers that flew over Europe. Images and slang names were commonly splashed across the tanks of their two-wheel steeds, just as they had been on the planes they piloted or crewed.

Stripped-down Harleys and Indians provided cheap thrills for the ex-GI looking for a little of the excitement left behind in the war, and they didn't mix well with the conservative, older AMA stalwarts. These were younger riders with little in the way of responsibilities, and who were looking to tavern hop, get a little juiced, and have some fun. With clubs boasting names like the Boozefighters and Coffin Cheaters, it is an understatement to say these guys were out for a little cruising and boozing.

So the stage was set for a boil-over, which happened at the 1947 Gypsy Tour, held during the Fourth of July weekend in the little Northern California burg of

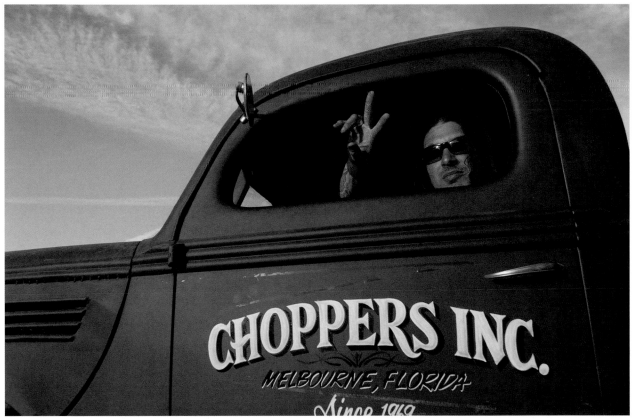

▲ Today, there are so many prominent chopper builders practicing so many widely varying styles that it's impossible to choose the dominant builder in the country. Billy Lane's retro-inspired creations make him a favorite of many. *Michael Lichter*

Hollister. All forms of riders and clubs showed up at this AMA-sanctioned event. Racing and drinking in the streets, bar brawls, confrontations with John Q. Law—it all blew apart in Hollister. These custom-bike riders came to America's consciousness when the news media showed up at Hollister to report the event. A "candid" picture showing a drunken biker on his Harley surrounded by broken beer bottles landed on the cover of *Life* magazine.

The 1954 film *The Wild One*, starring Marlon Brando and Lee Marvin, fictionalized the events of that night in Hollister. After its release, every biker became an outlaw biker. What began as a lot of young men releasing some pressure and finding themselves—but also wanting a little good-natured fun in the process—resulted in continual bad press that sealed the riders' reputation, even up to this day.

Thanks to the depiction of outlaw bikers in newspapers, movies, and television, bad bikers and their mad machines became the predominant images associated with motorcycling throughout the 1950s and '60s. California clubs like the Hell's Angels and Mongols unwittingly made sure the newspapers kept a spotlight on their activities throughout the 1960s. Even light fare like one of the mindless, mid-1960s Annette and Frankie beach movies, *Beach Blanket Bingo*, had Eric Von Zipper and his outlaw motorcycle gang doing some bad stuff.

But that was just the thing: choppers, as they were becoming to be known, did not go away. By the late 1960s, a groundswell of backyard manufacturers were looking to provide jockey shifts and sissy bars (to help support girlfriends' backs), and extended front forks for that Southern California chopper look. Soon after came the ape-hanger handlebars in dog-bone risers. The classic chopper was born.

▲ Ed "Big Daddy" Roth was *the* seminal purveyor of wacky kustom kars in the 1960s and a true American original. The fact that he went out on a limb to publish *Choppers Magazine* in the late 1960s is a testament to his role in helping to popularize the bikes.

▲ His willingness to experiment with radical and untried concepts has helped make Arizona's Paul Yaffe one of the most respected chopper builders in the United States. *Michael Lichter*

So where did the name "chopper" come from? Some have formulated a theory that it had to do with the rise in motorcycle thefts in the 1960s—in some cases by organized biker gangs peddling the stolen bikes and parts for a living. Stolen bikes could be significantly altered in "chop-shops," a term borrowed from clandestine automotive garages where stolen cars were stripped or "chopped up" and their parts sold to body and repair shops. The name was applied to the similar activities that motorcycle thieves were up to, and the term stuck.

Toward the end of the 1960s, a convergence of events established the foundation for the chopper phenomenon of today. In San Bernardino, California, Denver Mullins started Denver's Choppers, while in the shadow of Mickey Mouse, Anaheim's Tom McMullen started AEE Choppers as an extension of his small auto electric business. Both manufactured chrome sissy bars, big-inch motors, rigid frames, and more to feed the growing demand for chopper components. It seemed like anything they produced immediately sold out. These first manufacturing enterprises, combined with the release of the movie *Easy Rider* in 1969, fueled the image, philosophy, and look of the biker for all time.

Keying into the apparent popularity of the chopper craze, publications sprang up to bring the latest components, modifications, and culture via the mail or corner liquor store. No less than three bike publications from AEE's Tom

▲ Russ Tom's father was one of those returning World War II GIs who helped spawn the motorcycle boom in the United States. At a glance, Russ' bikes bear little resemblance to traditional choppers and bobbers, but his innovative Harley customs actually incorporate the best of the past and the future. *Michael Lichter*

McMullen—*Chopper, Street Chopper,* and *Hot Bike*—as well as Ed "Big Daddy" Roth's *Choppers Magazine,* filled the need for information. Movies and magazines were making choppers cool.

We all know that the kids of today become the buyers of tomorrow, and choppers seemed like a natural progression from Schwinn Sting-Rays of the 1960s and '70s and from Big Wheels of the 1970s and '80s. And so it continues. Today, the chopper mantra is being spread again, this time via popular television shows like *Motorcycle Mania* and *Monster Garage,* both starring West Coast Choppers' Jesse James, and *American Chopper,* featuring the father and son builders Paul Teutul and Paul Jr. There are so many prominent builders today, from Arlen Ness to Paul Yaffe and Billy Lane, that it is hard to keep track of who really is the dominant builder in the country. Furthermore, choppers really are not just an American occupation—countries around the world are embracing the custom-bike phenomenon and the outlaw reputation that comes with it.

Right now, we are in a period of rapidly developing styles and trends. For all we know, this may someday be considered the "golden age" of the custom bikes. So, if you have a motorcycle dream, you're not alone. Mastering this book won't bring that dream to reality, but at least you'll be able to take that dream from your brain to the drawing board. And that's the first step—which is one step further than most dreams ever get!

# Tools and Equipment

If you own pencils and paper, then you have the basic tools to draw anything. Actually, there are many tricks that will help you make your drawings and sketches easier to do and look more professional. One trick is to have a comfortable, well-lit work area and equipment that enhances your ability and makes it fun to draw choppers. Be forewarned: having this equipment without knowing the drawing basics won't help you a bit, just as the best bat, glove, and uniform do not make for the next Barry Bonds. This analogy holds true for computers, too (but more on that later). All of this equipment aids, but does not replace, your drawing abilities.

First off, you need a good drawing surface on which to work, like a solid table, desk, or drafting or light table. Whatever your decision, the key word is *sturdy*.

▶ You'll not only erase with these pencil-type erasers, you'll also create highlights and reflections by removing drawn or rendered material from your paper or board.

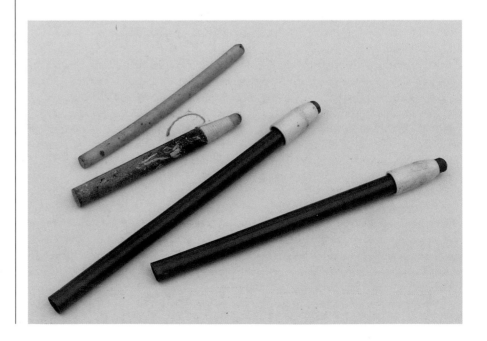

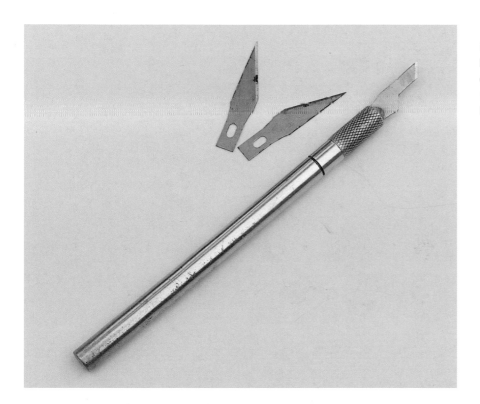

An X-ACTO knife is a must-have item for the budding artist. Different blades give you different types of control. The knife is used for cutting masks, scraping chalk for backgrounds, and much more.

Don't settle for one of those wobbly, bottom-of-the-line drafting tables with the hinge-and-catch brackets that have been known to amputate whole arms and hands (just kidding). If you need a surface that tilts, then a quality drafting table is your best bet.

Whatever drawing surface you work on, good lighting is a must, for obvious reasons. I like incandescent lighting, but you may wish to combine fluorescent and incandescent lights, or work under fluorescent conditions exclusively. Lighting should be even to avoid shadows or hot spots, so more than one source of light will probably spread out the light the best. I have three lamps at my drawing board. An articulating light is best for the occasional need to zone in for close-up work. Let's face it—you have to be able to see what you are doing, so start with a well-lit workspace.

As for your implement of choice, try experimenting with different types of pens and pencils until you find the one with which you are most comfortable. I base my choice of Verithin 747 black pencils on the fact that they smear less, put down a nice black line, and don't break as easily as a lead pencil. (I have a heavy hand.) Also, I find I have a bit more control with them; they tend to put out more resistance so my freehand line doesn't blast out of control over the paper. You may prefer the qualities that a No. 2 pencil offers, or a fine-tip pen, or even a ballpoint pen. I know people who sketch with all of them—even with a brush—and they all produce nice, "juicy" sketches.

If you use any type of wood pencil, you must have an electric pencil sharpener. Taking the time to sharpen a dull pencil with a hand-held sharpener after a few strokes is as annoying as your shovelhead regularly fouling plugs. And in such a circumstance, you are more likely to run with a dull pencil, which will produce marginal sketches at best. Why do you think they call them dull? Step up and get the electric sharpener so that you can flog away.

Once you start to tighten up your sketches, you'll want to look into templates and angles to help guide you and your pencil: 45-degree and 30/60-degree angles

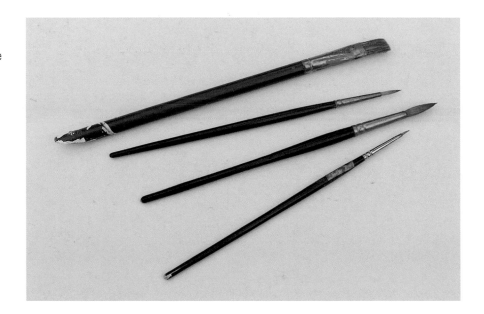

▶ A small assortment of brushes can be used not only for putting highlights into your drawings with white gouache, but also for actual drawing. Examples of this can be found later on in this book.

come in a variety of sizes, so choose which works best for you. Although the colored angles look cooler, stick with the clear ones, as it is easier to see your work through them.

Templates consist not only of the circle and ellipse variety, but also include French curves or "sweeps." Ellipse templates come in sets ranging from 10 to 80 degrees (with an ellipse, 100 degrees comprise a full circle). Sizes within this range go from 1/4 inch to 2 inches in the smaller template set. Start with this smaller set and see if you have any need for the larger sets, as they can be a bit pricey. The larger ellipse sets range in size from a 2- to 4-inch ellipse. They are great for larger drawings, but you may find you are more comfortable drawing smaller, in which case you will not need the larger set at all.

▶ Keep a can of Bestine handy for cleaning dirty sweeps and other instruments you gunk up with marker juice and pencil lead. It can also be used to create interesting backgrounds, like those depicted in the rendering sequence later in this book. A spray bomb of fixative works well to keep pencil or chalk down on your drawing, thus reducing instances of smudging. It also allows you to come back into the sketch and work in these sprayed areas later on.

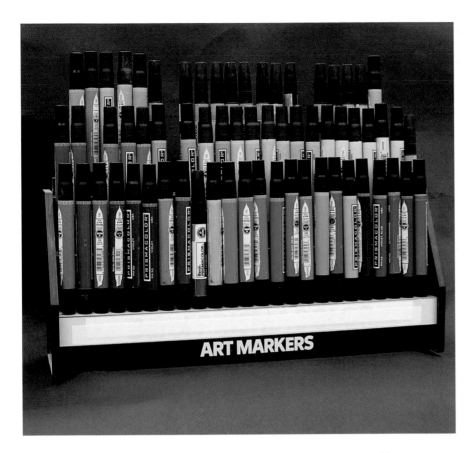

This is just one of the banks of colored markers I have to give me the widest range of colors and functions. Different brands of markers have pluses and minuses, so try a few different markers until you find the brand that works best for your needs. In terms of your health and the environment, the alcohol-based markers are better than the chemical-based ones. Lately, I have been able to find only the alcohol-based ones at the local art stores. If your local store is limited in their choices, try the Internet—where lots of art distributors sell their wares.

▲ There are lots of different fine-tipped pens and pencils to handle any fine drawing work you plan on doing. I tend to go for those that dry quickly so I don't smear the line work while it dries. Also with pencils, there are all kinds that "feel" and "mark" differently. Try out a few and see which one feels best to you.

▶ Good reference materials in the form of photos, clippings, magazines, and books are essential toward expanding your knowledge of choppers, as well as your visual library. In most cases, such references are rich sources for determining reflections, shadows, color, and light. They also can become a basis for going beyond reality once you start experimenting with your chopper renderings.

As for French curves or sweeps, they help in tuning up a line but should not be used as a replacement for freehand drawing, only as an enhancement! Most art stores, whether brick-and-mortar or online, carry a range of configurations from which to choose. Although the more complex and irregular curves look intriguing, try to find curves that display slight bows and gentle curves. These adapt better to chopper illustrations than the crazy-curve variety. I made my sweeps as a school project many moons ago. You can't buy them, but I've seen similar examples from time to time. They are about 20 inches long and work perfectly for motorcycle, car, and product design. Check out the photos and see if you can find something similar.

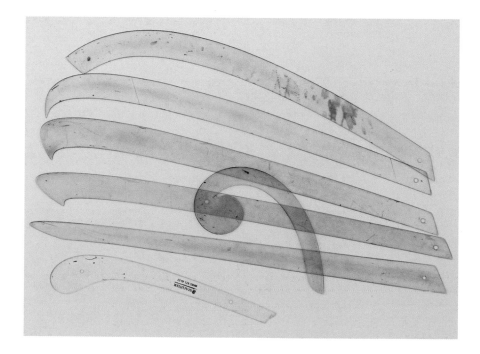

▶ To draw choppers, you might think an artist would need the most contorted and twisted set of sweeps available. It is just the opposite. The almost-straight sweep in the photo is the one I use the most. Because I made these particular sweeps, they are not available commercially. Try to find close duplicates.

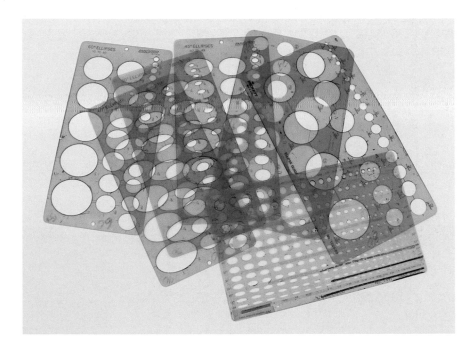

◀ Sets of ellipse templates are available in 10- to 80-degree ranges, as well as in a range of sizes. Start with the smaller set first, then see where your needs take you. Chapter Five is devoted to ellipses.

All of these plastic guides and templates get dirty from all of the marker juice, pencil lead, and chalk. A good solvent, like Bestine, dumped on a tissue works great for cleaning your smudged and dirty equipment. Do it often while you are in the middle of a drawing. Nothing looks worse than a smeared and dirty drawing caused by filthy hands and equipment. Don't be lazy—keep those hands and tools clean!

Other small but necessary items you need to have on hand are a variety of erasers. I prefer the Pink Pearl and white vinyl type in pencil form. You probably will have a specific area you wish to erase, and these thinner erasers get in a small area and do the job. The larger Pink Pearl and kneaded gray erasers take no prisoners. When you erase, they go for it all. Not good! Stick with those slender ones. They also work great for creating a highlight by erasing away a slight bit of your chalk or pencil. Slicing off the end gives you an incredibly sharp edge to render a nice, slim highlight. To get that clean slice, you'll need to purchase an X-ACTO knife. These razor-sharp knives have a variety of uses, but be careful—they slice through fingers and hands like they are butter!

Masking tape also comes in handy, but I prefer drafting tape because it sticks less, which helps save your latest creation from rips and tears while trying to peel up sticky masking tape. Drafting tape can also be used to mask off a drawing much like you would use Frisket or masking film. What's Frisket? It is a brand of thin, vinyl film with a slight adhesive backing on one side that you cut to a specific shape to protect or isolate an area around which you are working. Some artists even use it to protect their drawings from fingerprints and sweaty hands.

Finally, you'll need something on which to create your chopper drawings. Zillions of paper types and illustration boards are available to suit every desire. Start with a couple of different bond-paper tablets of at least 9x12 inches. You will find that paper varies in texture, thickness, and shades of white. Some take pencils better, while others take markers or chalk better. Experiment to see which type best fits your particular requirements. As we get into the actual drawing portions of this book, I will suggest certain types of paper or board that work well for the applications being discussed. But one of the real joys in drawing is tailoring your choices to what works best for you.

▼ These colored pencils go hand in hand with colored markers to help finish off those tight areas of your rendering, or to chisel in a particular line. Harder and slimmer than children's crayons, they are made of a similar wax base, but are able to create opaque areas. They can also be used to sketch with—especially when you get tired of black or dark blue drawings. A good range of these is a must!

# *Perspective*

Before you ride a chopper, you have to learn how to balance a bicycle. Well, this is the "balancing the bicycle" part of the book. I'm talking about perspective and its cousin: ellipses. I know this might be considered a bit boring, but you need it to draw anything— including wild choppers. You've got to admit it's very cool once you see that motorcycle sitting on your paper or board like it was a real 3-D object. You don't want to be drawing side views all of your life, so get through this chapter and apply what you learn to your next drawing. You've heard it before: you'll improve with some practice. So let's get going.

There is a mechanical way to draw in perspective, but it is a methodical process that does not allow for exaggeration or emphasis. Simple steps are covered in this chapter, but the best advice is to look with your eyes and brain. Try to visualize what it is you want to draw. Then use the ideas for perspective provided here

► When placing an as-yet-to-be-drawn object on a flat plane, the horizon line will dictate the view or eye level of your object. An artist represents linear perspective by pointing all lines in this imaginary space toward a vanishing point. The borders represent the limits to the space we are creating within it, and the rising sun represents the beginning of your journey to drawing choppers properly. Good luck!

HORIZON LINE

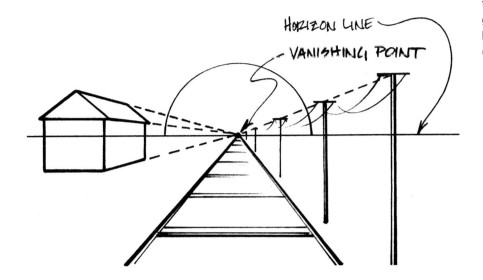

HORIZON LINE

VANISHING POINT

◀ Parallel, or one-point, perspective is best illustrated by the converging train tracks. Lines aimed at that point give the object and space the illusion of being 3-D. The dotted lines show that convergence.

to connect the eyes/brain part to these ideas. Relying on methods and plotting slows the drawing process and does not make for a fun drawing experience—and *fun* is what this is really about!

You have to make some decisions to begin. The first is to select how much of the front, side, or back of the chopper you wish to show. Usually, what is known as a "front 3/4 view" is most commonly chosen to draw or photograph a chopper because it gives the most information about the bike—in other words, the best sense of what the object looks like. Next, you must choose the viewer's (that's you) angle. Do you want to look down on the bike, as if from a high vantage point, or see it much like you would if you were walking along the street? Or as if you were on your hands and knees? Or from a worm's-eye view, or what is known as a "ground-level view"? The view you choose will determine the horizon line and vanishing points.

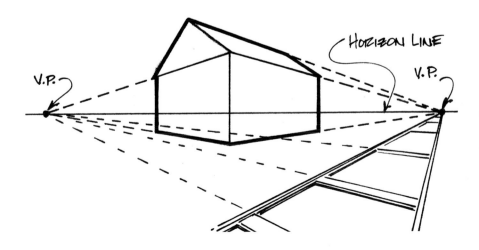

V.P.

HORIZON LINE

V.P.

◀ Lines that vanish in two directions illustrate angular, or two-point, perspective. This is a truer simulation of reality than the one-point perspective example and is the setup for virtually all bike depictions. As the objects go back into our space, they foreshorten. This means they shorten up because we actually see less as their sides angle away from us.

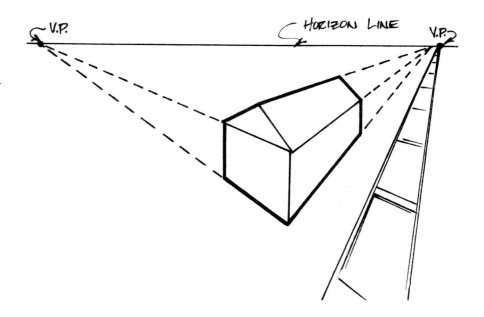

▶ Moving the horizon line to the upper portions of the space we have created yields a higher view than the previous example, which put the eye level right at the horizon line. This higher view is a good perspective to illustrate an interesting feature on the front of the bike and allows more view of the gas tank, seat, controls, and fenders.

The horizon line is that point out in the distance where the sky and ground meet. Hypothetically, you can see this line if it is a clear day and you are looking across an unobstructed stretch of desert or field. Obviously, the horizon line is rarely seen in real life because it is usually obstructed by smog, buildings, trees—you name it. Yet, if you are to construct an accurate drawing of a chopper and its surroundings, you need to draw or at least visualize this line. It is usually placed in the middle of the page, but its location determines how the bike is viewed. A low horizon line will result in a view as if you were high up looking down, a high horizon line will give you a worm's-eye view of the subject, and a line in between will logically give you a medium of these two extremes.

The vanishing point is that point at which the lines of a diminishing object disappear at the horizon line. But this description is a lot more confusing to

▶ A low horizon line gives you a low, or worm's-eye, view of the object. With the vanishing points within the space we have created, the object is given a very forced or extreme look.

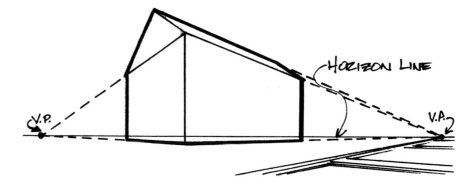

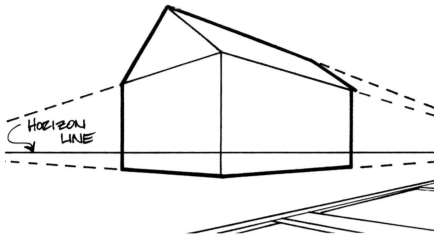

▲    A better solution may be to place the vanishing points outside the borders of our space. This gives a more realistic view of the object. You may want to practice placement of both the horizon line and vanishing points to see some of the different possible setups.

▼    Although not really applicable to drawing choppers, I thought I would at least clue you in on three-point perspective, a trick artists use when trying to give an object the sense of being very large. You see a lot of this used in comic books, where there is a lot of action and drama that needs to be conveyed within the panels of the stories.

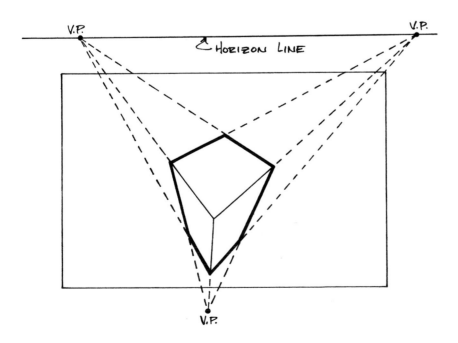

▶ This is the simplified chopper drawing that we are going to flip into perspective. The boxes around the tires are there to help you understand how we will turn a circle into perspective. The crosshairs represent the centers of those circles, which we will also see depicted in the perspective drawing of this bike. We'll delve into axes and ellipses in Chapter Five.

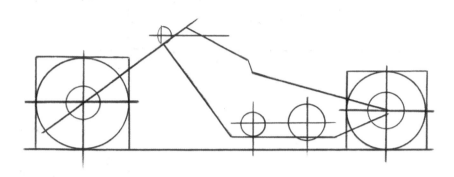

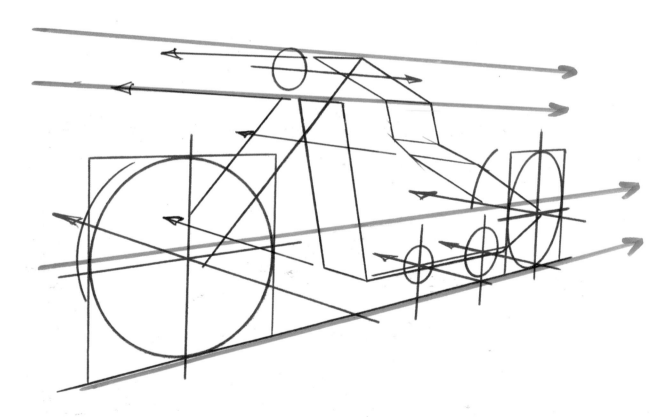

▲ Flipped into perspective, our chopper is seen in simplified planes, or a wire skeleton, with the horizon line close to the bottom portion of the neck. This drawing uses a two-point perspective, so the lines converging to one of our points are in green, and the lines going to the other point are in black with arrows to indicate the direction. The circles found on the bike are represented in blue and are now ellipses because they are in perspective. The red lines with arrows attached represent the major and minor axes of those ellipses, which we will get into in another chapter. You can see that as the green line converging to one point on the horizon gets closer to the horizon itself, and the black line pointing to the other vanishing point gets closer to the horizon line; they almost run over each other. Without it being indicated, you know that this is the horizon itself.

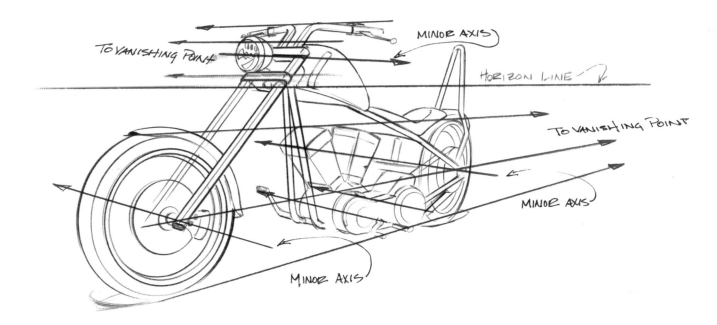

Converting our simplified skeleton into an actual chopper drawing, the red lines indicate the converging lines of the two vanishing points; those red lines running through the center of the ellipses represent the minor axes, which are pointing to their respective vanishing points. Again, we'll see what this is all about in Chapter Five. Below the horizon line the converging lines are angled up to it, and above the horizon our lines are angled down to it. This is a classic 3/4 front-view drawing with a basic horizon line about midway through the middle of the object.

▲ Bobbers, hot rods, and customs—our three favorite things . . . almost! Where is the horizon line on this cool Keith Weesner drawing? Yes, it is at the top of the drawing. If you answered this question correctly, you may continue with this chapter. If not, you must read it over again—I mean it!

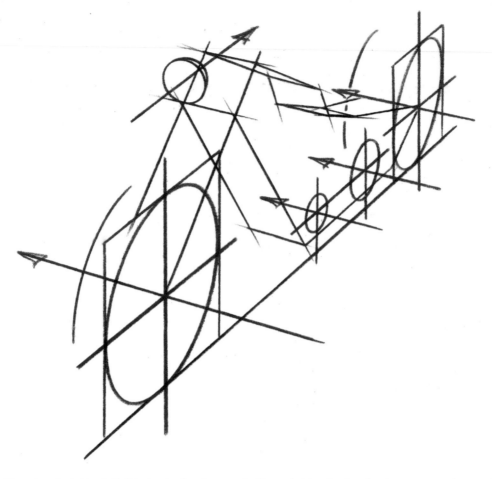

▲  If we tried to replace the bobber in Keith's drawing (previous page) with our skeleton drawing, the planes, axes, and converging lines would look like this. Every line is headed up to the two points Keith created on the horizon line.

understand than the simple example of train tracks, whose vanishing point is where the tracks come together out in the distance at the horizon line.

There are really only two types of vanishing point setups with which you need to concern yourself. The first is the one-point perspective, where only one vanishing point is used. The railroad track scenario fits this example best. Next is the two-point perspective, which is the usual method used for drawing bikes. Rather than describe it here, the accompanying examples will help you better understand this concept.

Objects in perspective lose detail and value as they go back into the atmosphere of the imaginary space you have created in your sketch. Atmosphere softens the details and lightens the values. To create perspective and visually pull an object toward you, adding more detail and value are two of several things you can do to trick the eye. This actually works in the artist's favor, because it becomes unnecessary to put as much effort into the detail of objects farther back in perspective. Since choppers are short objects compared to cars, buildings, or city streets, decreased detail and value don't factor in as much as they do with bigger objects, but are worth keeping in mind as a trick for creating reality and depth in the drawing.

I talk about value here and throughout the book. Value refers to the lightness or darkness an object exhibits either in color or in black and white. Pastel colors,

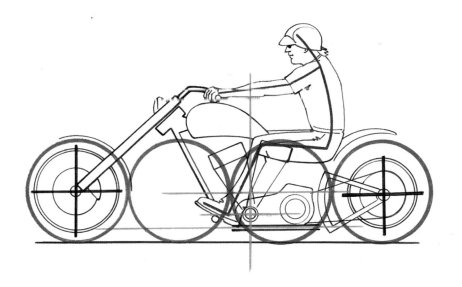

With four tires we get a more "custom" look, or stance, to our bike. Customs tend to have raked necks that kick the front tire out and retain the low or level relationship of the bike to the ground. The handlebars come back to the rider, who is in a more reclined position. Note that the rider is sitting down into the bike more than on our bobber (facing page). Also, look at the location of the engine. The green guidelines help to indicate its position in relation to the red tire guides.

bobbers to customs to old-school choppers and more. This is also the reason why we see so many variations in design and proportion within each of these categories.

In this chapter, we will discuss guidelines for laying out the framework or foundation for your chopper—which really comes down to proportion. Paying attention to this will partially determine whether it looks right or wrong. And one of the easiest ways to ascertain whether you are on the mark in terms of proportion is to scale your chopper to an element of itself.

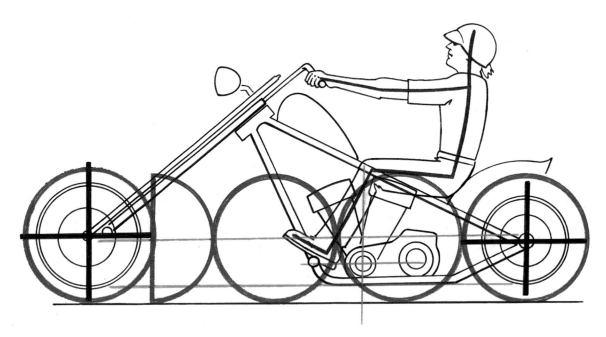

What a difference a bit more tubing has on the proportion of this classic chopper. Extended frame, radically raked neck, extended forks—it's the look! The rider is leaning back, with arms locked into a straight position. The rider and engine are generally in the same position and location as the custom. Note, also, that the bottom of the frame is parallel with the ground. The whole frame could be raked up further for an even wilder chopper stance. As you can see, once you pick up on the proportions of your favorite bike, it is fun to jack around with the positions of the rider and the elements of the bike itself. Now check out the sketching chapter to see how we take this information and turn our boring side view into a different perspective!

We'll try to do the same thing we did on our chopper to a person. Let's face it, most drawings you do will want to incorporate a rider, so you'll need this information to create the most accurate "scene" that you can. Our buddy "Bob" averages out to be about seven and one-half heads tall, with about three heads of shoulder width. These proportions may be a bit like the proportions of the Incredible Hulk, but we don't want a wimpy chopper rider, do we? Note that the waist is about at the third head, and that the crotch is about four heads down—not quite in the middle of "Bob." The knees are at about the sixth head. If we really wanted Bob to be tall, we might make him a full eight heads high.

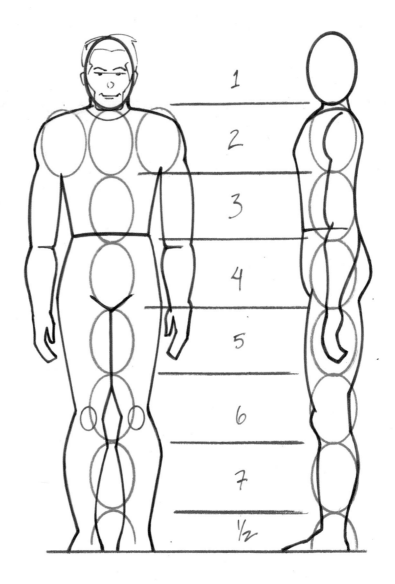

Huh?

Well, you know that the two tires are basically the same diameter, or size. These can be used as a means to scale your drawing—in other words, to roughly measure dimensions. We're not talking about an accurately scaled diagram, just a quick-and-easy way to see if you are in the range of acceptability with the proportions you have chosen to draw. It's an aid that is both fun and easy.

An example: on the average, a chopper is about four tires long, with the engine placed a bit back from the middle of your four-tire proportion. The height is usually not more than a tire and a half—unless you want to run ape hangers for handlebars. Armed with this information, you now have an aid to help spin the bike around into perspective and have it turn out in proportion. For information on how to incorporate the proportion you create into a perspective drawing, see Chapter Six, where the concepts explained here are translated into a perspective drawing of your favorite chopper.

We can even do this when drawing a person by segmenting off a person based on the size of his head. Again, we are using a part of the object and relating it to the rest of it in order to draw in proportion. Try it out and see if you get the hang of it. The more you sketch, the more you will find that you can see the proportion of the object with your eye. Once you master proportion, it's time to break all of the rules and play around with what a different proportion does for a chopper. Or you may want to break the rules to create a cartoon. Exaggerating proportion is one of the first things relied upon to turn a drawing into a cartoon, whether you exaggerate the rider, the bike itself, or both. There is a whole chapter on cartoons later in this book that shows plenty of liberties of proportion used to create some cool cartoons. That's one of the great things about drawing: once you learn some rules, it's fun to break them and see what you can make work.

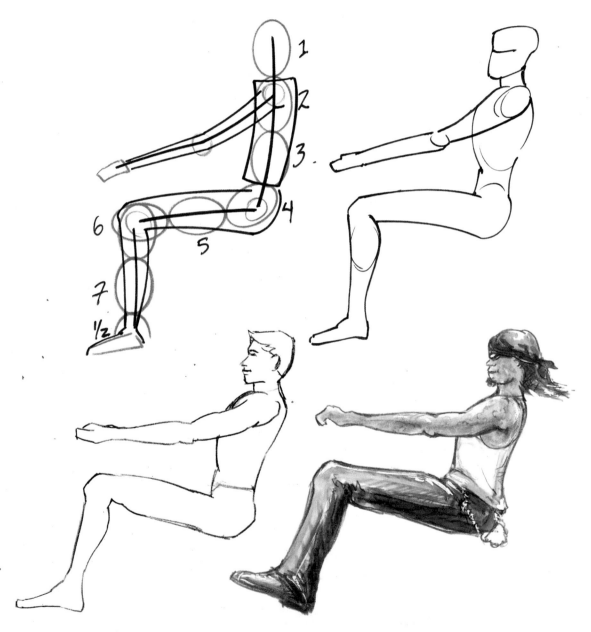

▲    Now, let's turn Bob into a biker! First, we apply what we have mapped out to position Bob on a bike. As we progress, we smooth out the contours and define muscle and bones. Adding some details and color, a "wife beater" shirt, a chain, and some hair, Bob now has the biker look. What, no tats? Look closely—they're on the arm!

# Ellipses and Axes

The most common mistake I see in drawings of any kind is the incorrect placement of round or cylindrical objects in perspective, yet it is the simplest theory in practice. I guess it is not covered much in art classes. Or perhaps those without a firm grasp of the concept do not bother to analyze how to put a round object into perspective. Whatever the reason, choppers are full of cylindrical and round objects, so there is no getting around this. Now pay attention!

This really is another easy method to pick up. Quite simply, an ellipse is just a circle in perspective. As you will see in examples throughout the book, the keys to putting a tire, primary, or brake into perspective are the major and minor axes of the ellipse. That, and an intelligent eye, should work every time. The one point to remember is that, except on a football, there are no points on a cylindrical object

▶ Since it is easy to put a box into perspective, this is how we will begin to help us place circular objects like tires, wheels, and headlights into our 3-D imaginary space. The dot represents the center of the box in the first example, and the perspective center of the box in the second example. When the circle is placed into perspective, it becomes an ellipse. Notice that the ellipse is a continuous curve and that there are no points at the tight ends of the ellipse.

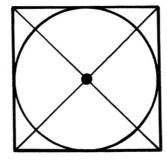

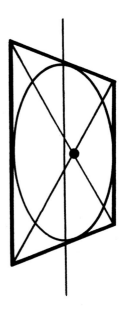

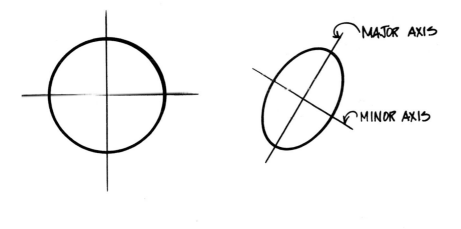

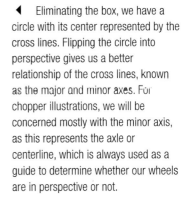

Eliminating the box, we have a circle with its center represented by the cross lines. Flipping the circle into perspective gives us a better relationship of the cross lines, known as the major and minor axes. For chopper illustrations, we will be concerned mostly with the minor axis, as this represents the axle or centerline, which is always used as a guide to determine whether our wheels are in perspective or not.

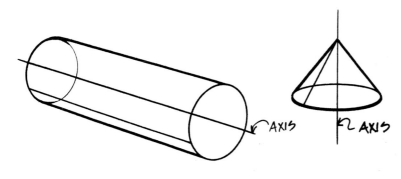

Creating a cylinder, or cone, relies on the minor axis. In the cone's case, its point rests somewhere on the minor axis, depending on how tall you would like to make it. For our cylinder, the minor axis determines its far end, or end cut. Since the cylinder is going back into perspective, we have to converge our sides slightly, which means our far-end ellipse will be slightly smaller than our front one. Got it?

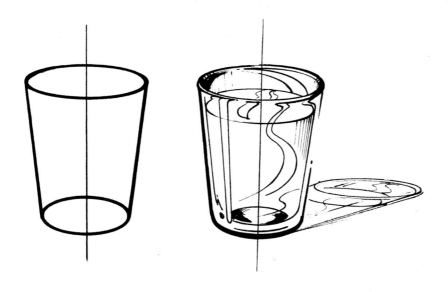

Again, the minor axis is the guide from which we create a cocktail glass. Notice how the bottom ellipse is less pinched than the top one. This is because as we move down on the glass and away from the horizon line, we see more of the bottom.

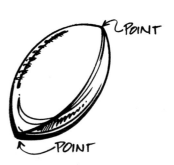

in perspective! A tin can, bowl, or tire lying on its side—none of these objects have pointy ends. You will see it a lot in drawings and paintings, but it is *wrong*. Trust me on this!

With this in mind, refer to the drawings in this chapter for simple methods and aids to help you nail down this final technical part before we move on to some less technical aspects of drawing choppers.

Only footballs have points in perspective!

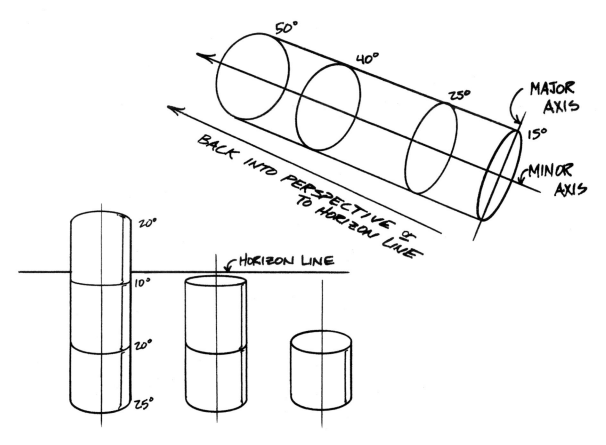

▲   Ellipses are identified by degrees, with the tightest being almost zero, which would be represented by a line and not an ellipse. A full circle is 100 degrees, represented by a true circle. As mentioned with the cocktail glass drawing, as circular objects move away from the horizon line, their degree of roundness becomes larger. A circle sitting on the horizon line becomes a line, or zero degree, while moving above or below the horizon line yields a larger-degree ellipse, increasing in size the farther you go.

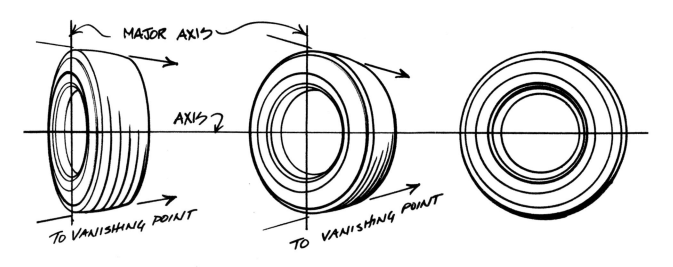

▲   A combination tire/wheel assembly is just a series of built-up ellipses. The vanishing points will dictate the angle that the face of the tire tread takes. Because the axis represents the center of the bike's axle, it becomes the predominate concern when constructing a tire/wheel combination for your chopper drawing.

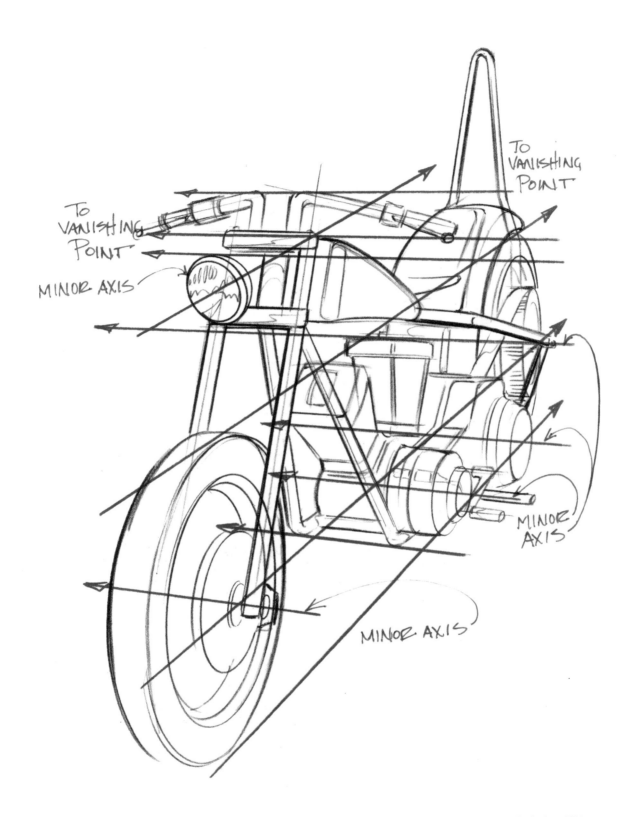

TO VANISHING POINT

TO VANISHING POINT

MINOR AXIS

MINOR AXIS

MINOR AXIS

▲ Whether it is the headlight, wheels, primary, or shifter peg, every minor axis heads toward the vanishing point on the horizon. With a good eye, you may be able to determine the degree of the ellipse you wish to use. In our example, the front wheel/tire is a 25- or 30-degree ellipse. As the circles work their way back into perspective, they get tighter, ending with a 10- or 15-degree ellipse for the rear wheel and pulley. Also note that although the left side controls are cylindrical, they are directly in front of the viewer, so they have no perspective and become merely straight lines. Because viewers have the rest of the bike as reference, they will know that they are round.

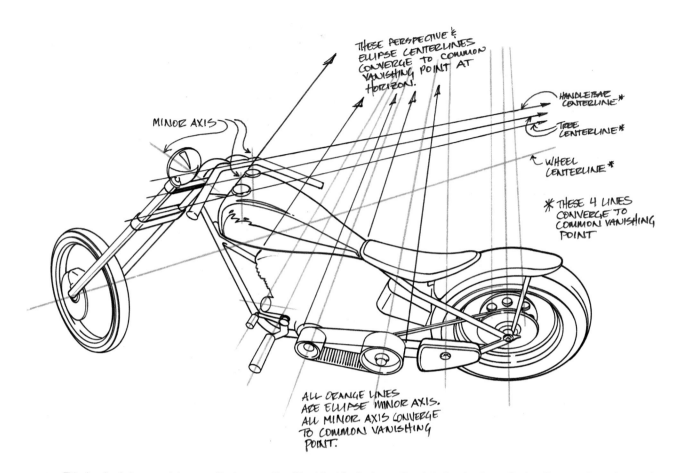

THESE PERSPECTIVE &
ELLIPSE CENTERLINES
CONVERGE TO COMMON
VANISHING POINT AT
HORIZON.

HANDLEBAR
CENTERLINE *

TREE
CENTERLINE *

WHEEL
CENTERLINE *

* THESE 4 LINES
CONVERGE TO
COMMON VANISHING
POINT

MINOR AXIS

ALL ORANGE LINES
ARE ELLIPSE MINOR AXIS.
ALL MINOR AXIS CONVERGE
TO COMMON VANISHING
POINT.

▲   This drawing is in one-point perspective because the side of the bike is almost directly facing the viewer. So, just like our train track example, all of the lines converge to one point on the horizon. Or do they? What we really have is a situation of one object with two separate segments, or planes, sort of like an articulating bus or a train with its separate cars. Each of these segments—in this case, the front tire/fork and then the rest of the bike—has its own perspective. The black lines represent the convergence toward each of the plane's vanishing points, and the orange lines are the minor axes for the ellipses. If I had drawn this with the forks turned perfectly straight, then the entire bike would have been drawn in one-point perspective. I have included the minor axes for the gas caps and headlight. The headlight axis is based on the same plane as the forks, and the axes for the gas caps go with the top plane of the tank. Do a rough sketch of your favorite chopper and try placing circular objects on it to practice this theory.

# Sketching and Line Quality

Sketching techniques, in many ways, are like signatures and are just as varied. The way a drawing is sketched can identify who did the work. Later, I'll get into the different types of drawing tools and how they can change an artist's style. Here, I'll provide some examples and suggestions for you to develop and try out yourself. The ability to sketch should come easily, so some of these suggestions may be too cumbersome for your taste. Not to worry. Use what you can from this chapter, or try to adapt some of these suggestions to your own style of drawing.

The main objective is to have fun and stay loose when you draw or sketch. A relaxed and free hand and drawing from your whole arm—even your whole body—instead of quick rips from the wrist, help you maintain a nice flow in your

◀ Keith Weesner has been around hot rods and customs all of his life. Over the last few years he has developed his unique style to portray the hot rod and biker lifestyles in commercial as well as fine art. Thumbnail sketches like this are never meant to be seen; they are merely tools for the artist to develop his drawing. Keith was kind enough to provide some of his thumbnails, which show his early thoughts—basically trying to get what he sees in his brain onto paper. This sketch exhibits loose, bold strokes. The ellipses are not round and there are no straight lines, yet it is a nice sketch where we can clearly see the whole bike and, in some cases, in great detail.

From this single crude thumbnail came a show bike from one of the preeminent chopper builders around: Arlen Ness. He asked me for some rough sketches of an idea we had talked about, and from this simple sketch he created the *Sled* bike. How cool is that? How valuable was my ability to do a quick, clean sketch for Arlen?

drawings and achieve more controllable lines. You've seen the "chicken scratch" style of drawing with short, quick strokes and jabs. My observations and practice of different drawing styles have shown me that this style can be very distracting and less professional. You may want to pay particular attention to the way lines are delineated and also their weights and emphasis.

Line weights are the thickness and thinness of lines that make up a sketch. Variations in line weight hold the viewer's attention longer because they are a lot more interesting to look at than lines that are consistent. From the artist's standpoint, they are also more fun to create and are probably easier and quicker to do

▲ Let's try a simple side-view sketch, and then flip it around and draw it in perspective. This is how I started, with this thumbnail. Because I was designing the bike, I needed to work out the frame configuration, tank, and general proportions before I started to do a more finished sketch. It is extremely crude, but as we have already seen, someone like Arlen Ness could actually build a bike from this.

than a drawing with repetitive, rigid line weight throughout. Typically, you give more emphasis, or line weight, to a line that is closer to you; a line that helps to represent an undercut edge; an edge that defines something round; or a part of a drawing that calls for some extra pressure. After all, drawing is as much a tactile experience as it is a visual one.

A great sketch contains lots of different line weights that contribute to what is referred to as line quality. Don't get bogged down by common weights. Give your drawing some spark and interest by varying those weights. You'll see and feel the difference.

▲   This is the first workout where I determine realistic proportions (see Chapter Four). Basically I drew a circle, then three other circles next to it to help set up boundaries, or landmarks, to build up the drawing. Sketching a centerline through the wheels, I placed the engine almost in the middle of the bike, both horizontally and vertically. Again I'm trying to figure out my landmarks for proportion purposes. All of the lines are light at this stage so that if I need to change something, I can just draw over what I have already done instead of erasing and then drawing over it.

▶ The wheels, engine, and primary established my landmarks to draw in the unconventional frame. From there, I was able to create the neck, handlebars, and oil tank location. Because I kind of knew where I was at, I was able to draw the frame a bit tighter and bolder. It then became the foundation for building the rest of the bike on my paper.

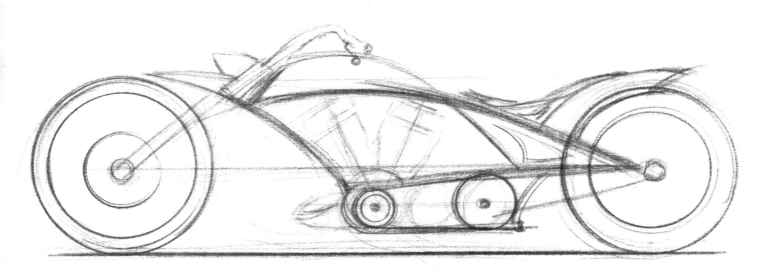

▲ Sketching in the fenders and seat, I also came back in with a circle template to hammer in the tires and pulleys. This is starting to look like a real bike!

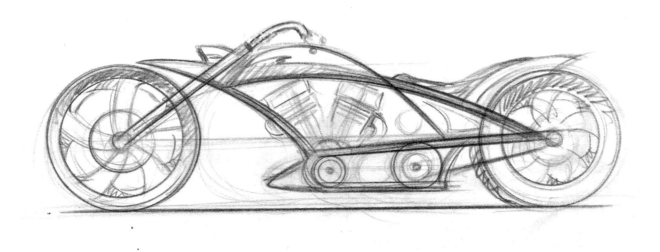

▲  A funky wheel design, some shading, and reflection in the tank, and I'm ready to put this dude into perspective.

▲  To start our perspective drawing, we need to set up the horizon and general proportions of the bike, based on the side-view sketch I just created. This sketch will put our eye level right in the middle of the bike, so we don't have to be as concerned with vanishing points. Remember why? Our line through the middle of the wheels represents the point from which we will build the sketch. It becomes the horizon line, the approximate middle of the bike, the location of the minor axes, and it helps locate the engine. Once this is established, I draw in my four ellipses, making them slightly fuller as they get closer to the viewer. From there, I try to place the engine and try to draw in a lot of its elements. I have placed it a little farther back from where it was drawn on the side-view sketch because once I visualized the primary and pulleys relative to the rear wheel, it just needed to come back a bit.

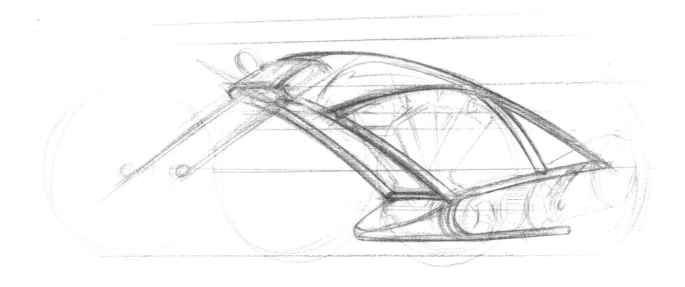

▲   With the engine and wheel locations established, I could sketch in the frame, which works its way around the primary and rocker boxes of the engine. That led me to put in the neck and forks, tank, and air foil hangin' out front.

▲   At this stage we are basically building up the bike, because we know where each of the components goes in relation to the components that have already been drawn. In some ways, it is like building an actual bike, component by component, except without the sweat, mess, and cost.

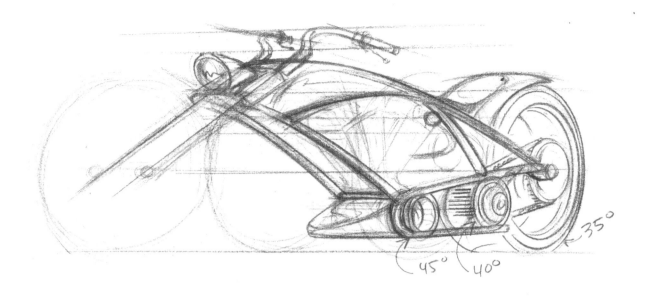

▲   Truing up the ellipses tightens up the drawing—at least for me. So I came back with my ellipse templates and hammered in the tire/wheel, drive pulleys, and headlight ring.

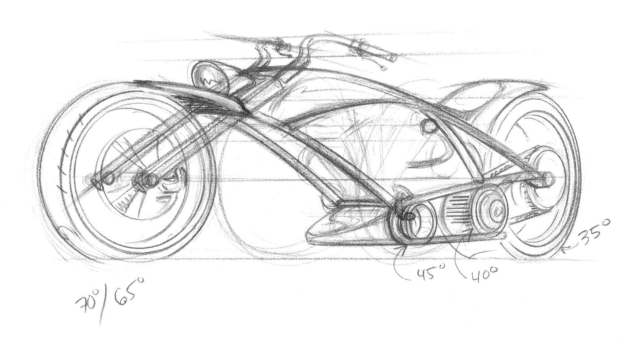

▲   I did the same thing to the front, including the disc brake. With some other piddling around and blocking in a front fender, I was done with this drawing. From here I could use this as an underlay to do a tighter color rendering, or use it as a basis for modifying my experimental frame design still further. If it were a little cleaner I could consider erasing some of the errant lines and guides and making it a bit better, but still, it is good enough to get an idea of how this bike would look for real.

▶ Here's another Keith Weesner workout—an initial sketch to get the proportions and design elements down on paper. Keith obviously likes Trumpets.

▼ From that crude start Keith has used a brush to draw up a more finished piece with more detail and shading. Keith likes to do his drawings with a lot of contrast—in other words, dark darks and light lights.

▲    Keith's finished drawing has a lot more detail and finer line work. He has even made some changes to the monster tank and exhaust pipes. Because he took this drawing in steps, Keith had the latitude to make changes along the way. Most cool drawings you see were not magically drawn up in one sketch, but rather in a series of sketches.

BIKE-TRUCK

CAPT. PEE PEE

46

◀ Ed Newton loves to design, and when he does, his thumbnails are done on whatever he has lying around—in this case notebook paper. His technique is nice and juicy, with his use of light and dark line work emphasizing some portions of the sketch and playing down others. This makes the drawing interesting because he varies his line weights.

◀ From the initial sketches on the facing page, Ed zeroed in on a design that both he and his client—in this case Ed "Big Daddy" Roth—liked, and then created a tighter drawing. Note his use of perspective guidelines. Yes, we *all* need to do that! Also note the dark areas coming from the back side of the paper. This is chalk that he put down to transfer the image onto illustration board.

◀ Once transferred, Ed inked it in for the final, done without gradations, so that it could be used on T-shirts and printed material. With the play of darks and lights, this becomes a very punchy drawing.

'STRANGE LOVE'

▲ As a design study, John Bell uses black pen to jot down his ideas. He builds up the drawing, going fairly light at first and then darkening the lines he wants to emphasize. He'll also do some light sketching to indicate objects in shadow, or those in the distance, like the rider's left leg and shoe. And if you look closely, there are a lot of little guidelines that John uses to help guide him through the sketch.

Some artists use sketchbooks to put down ideas when the inspiration strikes. Here, Keith Weesner has put down an image he wants to consider for a future sketch or painting. Is it rough? A little, but it is not meant to be seen, and really, it has all of the information he needs to decide whether he wants to develop it further. We have been fortunate enough that quite a few of the artists in this book have let us see some of the preliminary stuff they normally don't show anybody. In some cases, it is actually more interesting than the final piece.

Here is another sketch from Keith Weesner that was used to create the final painting shown on the next spread. Although there were other sketches leading up to the final, this was Keith's inspiration for the painting. The simple, quick sketch basically lays down the final composition he will use, though many small details were changed around.

Weesner '04

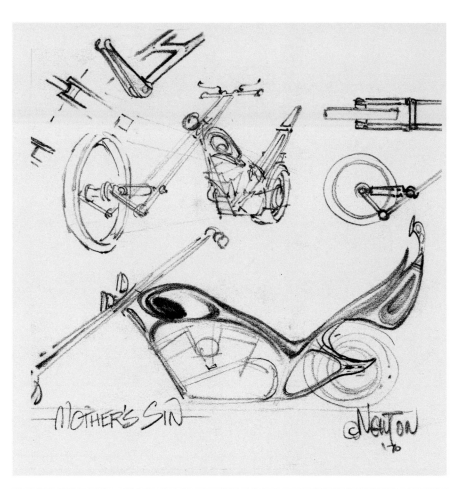

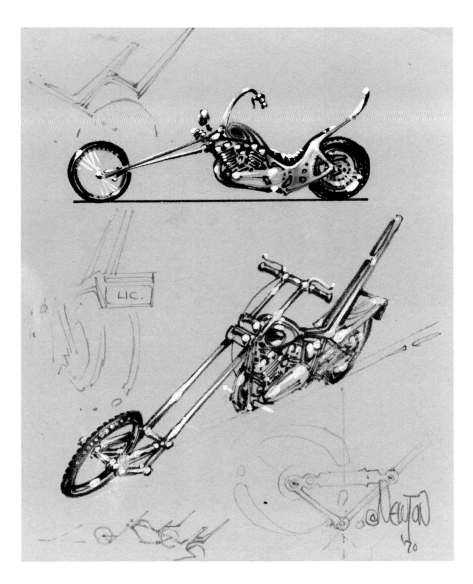

Some more notebook sketches from the mind of Ed Newton. These are over 30 years old. They show a general progression of this design, ending up as more developed sketches done on colored paper with white gouache thrown in to help delineate and highlight. Once you are able to translate your ideas from head to paper, it really becomes a lot of fun to sketch all the different ideas floating around in your brain.

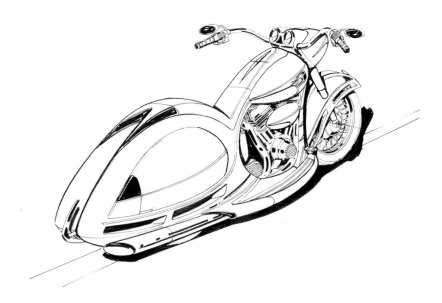

Don Varner is a Northern California designer who started out in the 1950s as a well-known Bay Area pinstriper. He has been involved with a number of very cool custom Harleys for Bob Dron, owner of Harley-Davidson of Oakland. One of the most well known of their collaborations was the *Royale*. Varner works very large—this very clean sketch that Varner created for the project is done on 18x24-inch paper. The line work is very controlled and clean, with Don using sweeps to keep the drawing precise. Thick and thin line work makes this sketch really rich.

7 8/94

'SE·II                    PRELIMINARY    SKETCH

Two more Don Varner sketches—these done almost entirely in marker. I've seen marker sketches over the years that have a real scratchy, amateur look. Don's marker sketches for Bob Dron are clean and controlled, with a nice blending of color. You can't do blends like this with dry markers—they need to be nice and juicy! Don starts with very fine pen lines, and then comes back with quite heavy lines and blended color. These are from the same series of sketches, but note the design differences between the two. These aren't just nice sketches—they're working tools to determine design direction.

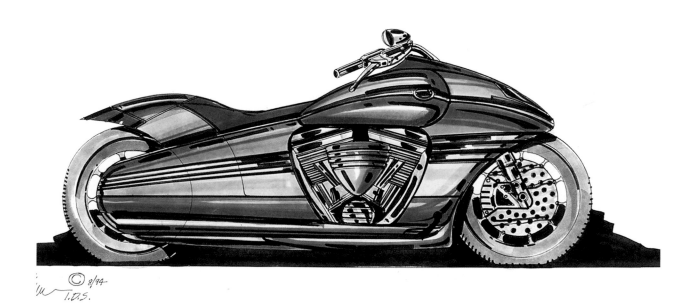

© 8/94
T.D.S.

# *Light Source*

When dealing with shading, coloring, shadows, and even where to place certain line emphasis in a line drawing, the light source that is cast on your subject is very important. Light helps define the components of your chopper, as well as where it is in perspective. And the color of the light source can add a whole new way to dramatically render your subject.

Generally, the lightest portion of the drawing is where the greatest amount of light is cast on the subject. The light values then get progressively darker as the surfaces move away from the core source of the light. Areas in shade are reserved for the darkest values. The easiest way to help you with this is to remember the

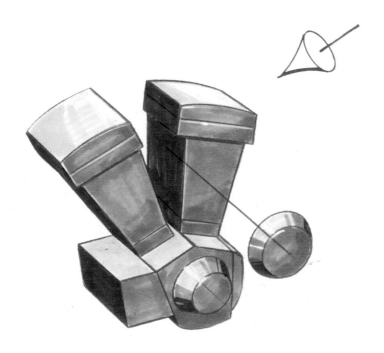

◀ This is an Evo-type engine broken down into basic shapes. Even though there are numerous cooling fins, nuts, brackets, and other details, this is the basic parameter for lighting the engine when the light source is from the direction shown. The top No. 1 surfaces are the lightest, the sides of the engine toward the light source are the No. 2 surfaces, and the sides away from the source are No. 3.

55

▶ Same engine, same side, same light direction, but different view of the engine itself. With the light source being somewhat behind the engine, we lose the opportunity to highlight the part of the engine we see the most. We also can't cast highlights over the fins of the cylinders, the rocker boxes, air cleaner, and other components. With the light source pulled closer toward you (the viewer), we would be able to sparkle up that cool V-twin, the gas tank, and all of the other components we would see in the drawing.

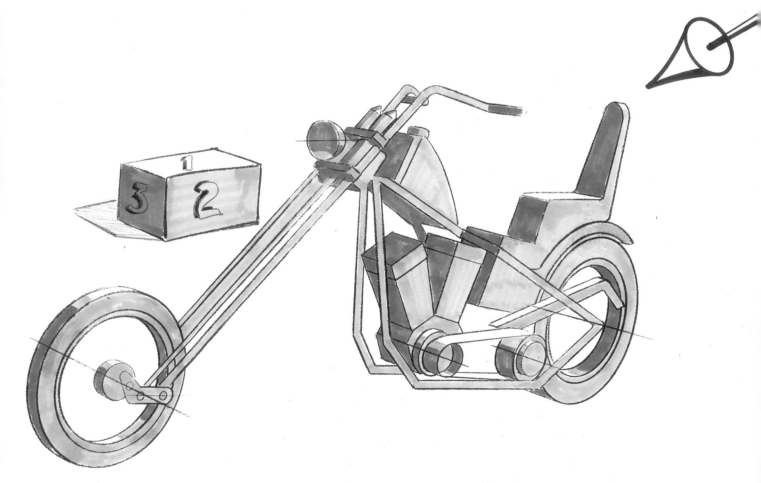

▲ In my opinion, this is the optimal lighting location for this simplified chopper drawing. The one-, two-, three-box theory used to the left tells the story: the majority of the light is on the top and the side that the viewer can see the most. If the light source was down a bit, you would have the opportunity to highlight a little more of the side, which might be a little better.

▲ Same chopper, different light source. As you can see, less of the bike is in the No. 1 and No. 2 light value. Because we want to try to get the most light on our subject for the best effect, another source location would be advised.

"one-, two-, three-box theory." The top of the box is your lightest (No. 1) value because the sun casts its strongest rays at the top of your object, right? The side of the box that is closest to the light source is the No. 2 side, while the side receiving the least amount of light is the No. 3 (or darkest) side. This is one of those basic rules you must not forget!

Nature has given you a dark base from which to visually support your chopper by means of the dark shadow cast below it. A warning: keep your light source in the general area of your head. Sure, you can cast light from the right or left side of your subject, but not from the behind. I mean you can do that, but lighting from the rear eliminates the light and the concentrated values reflected as highlights on your bike, which only allows you to use a restricted range of values on the bike's components. In addition, it casts a big, ugly shadow of your chopper right in front of it, which can draw the viewer's eye to the shadow instead of the subject. You don't want the shadow to become the big, bad hole into which the bike is poised to fall.

To take the position of the lighting source one step further, try to cast it on whatever side of the bike it is most advantageous to define. In other words, if you are drawing a front 3/4 view of a chopper from the left side, you may want to cast the light source more from the right side of your paper. This will allow you to cast it along the entire side of your chopper, yet still give you a bit of light to highlight portions of the front. Or, you may prefer lighting from the left to give you the opportu-

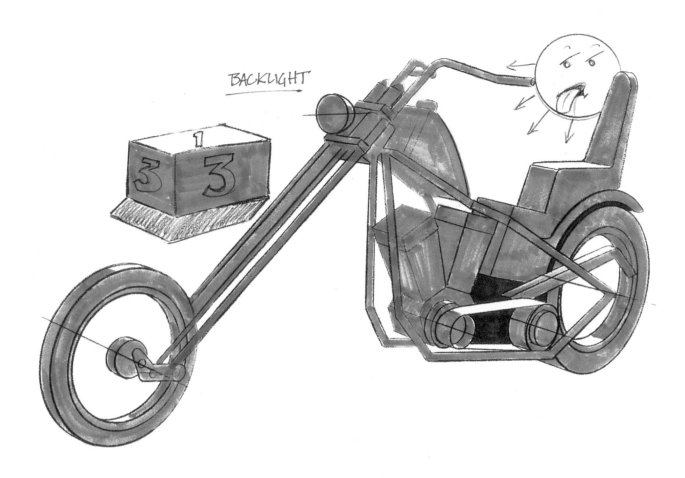

BACKLIGHT

▲ With the light source to the back of the bike, the entire chopper is in shade, or No. 3, value. What I haven't indicated is the big, ugly shadow that would be cast in front of the bike, taking your eye away from the subject. Don't do this!

nity to cast light along the front, picking up all of the highlights that headlights, forks, and springer front ends allow. You see, the light source is merely another tool you can use to help define the bike. You control it for your drawing's greatest benefit.

Recall from Chapter Three how objects become lighter in value and possess less detail toward the back of the imaginary space created in your drawing? This is somewhat contrary to the fact that as you move farther away from a light source, things get progressively darker. Yet if you observe mountain ranges stepped back, from a visual sense the mountains that are the closest appear darker and come forward. You may want to play with this phenomenon on paper to see what it does.

# *Shadows and Reflections*

Rendering chrome or shiny reflections on a drawing is, for me, probably the most enjoyable part of doing the sketch. Knowing how to do it properly takes a certain amount of practice, along with constantly observing exactly what happens to the bike's surfaces in the real world. When dealing with reflections, you must remember that your reflections should not look like stripes or blobs painted on the chopper. They should look like . . . well, reflections. Before you start to render in your reflections, a good way of looking at the task at hand is to keep in mind that the bike's surfaces are really just one huge mirror reflecting what is around it. Carefully observe the surfaces, visualize what is reflected into them, and

◀ This sketch by computer wizard Jim Bruni pretty much summarizes this whole chapter. Simple reflections for the shiny surfaces, softened reflections for the less reflective surfaces, and straightforward shadows for both the board racer and the Cyclone lettering behind the main image. Also note that the lettering in the tank continues the reflection running through the tank. If the lettering stayed the same value throughout, it would look like something pasted onto the top of the rendering. By picking up the reflection in the tank, the lettering looks as real as the bike itself.

▲    A simple side-view sketch I did that limits the amount of colors used, the amount of reflections, and probably reality as well! However, the point is that if you are timid about reflections, you can block in color and still get a reasonable sketch by layering in the color. That means stepping the color from lighter to darker values, or vice versa, as opposed to blended gradations. A touch of pencil work helps to blend out the harsh color breaks on components that reflect less. Finally, don't forget to drop shadows in where appropriate. This was an attempt to do the most with the least amount of gradations and color. How did I do?

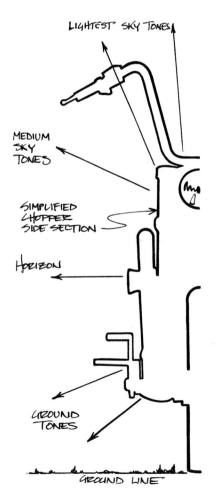

▶    Think of a chopper as a giant, convoluted mirror reflecting everything around it. This becomes another element of the space you are creating when you begin to draw your motorcycle. Where is it? What is sitting around it? Where is the light source? You set the stage for your drawing, and you create that stage to best define your chopper. Also, your chopper drawing is picking up reflections, but it is also picking up cast colors like cool shades from the sky, warm colors from the ground, and highlights from the compression of the light source at surface changes. We'll touch on that soon in this chapter.

you have the basis for your reflection patterns.

Although I will show some step-by-step examples in this chapter, there are a few ways you can train yourself to sketch reflections into any surface you choose. The first and best way is to observe. It may be an obvious thing to suggest, but a chopper's surface changes continuously. Observe the reflections dancing over the bike's surfaces to see how they react to changes in direction, surface shapes, sculpturing, indentions, etc. Keep a sketchpad with you and draw what you see for future use. Also seek out a good reference source, such as a magazine, that shows an example of a reflection, freezing in time the way a particular surface changes in response to what is around it.

Combine your observations and reference material, try a simple thumbnail sketch on scratch paper until you are satisfied with what you see, and then apply that to your real

◀ What is reflected on your chopper? All of what is shown here and more. Anything you wish to reflect is fair game—just make sure you don't confuse the viewer or yourself. If you do, your drawing will end up looking like the dinner in Fluffy's cat bowl. Most of the examples in this book tend to simplify the expanse around the bike. Its components—especially tubing—usually compress and stretch out reflections so that the horizon becomes merely a thin, dark line reflected onto the surfaces of the bike. And with tubing, everything becomes stretched out and turns into thin lines.

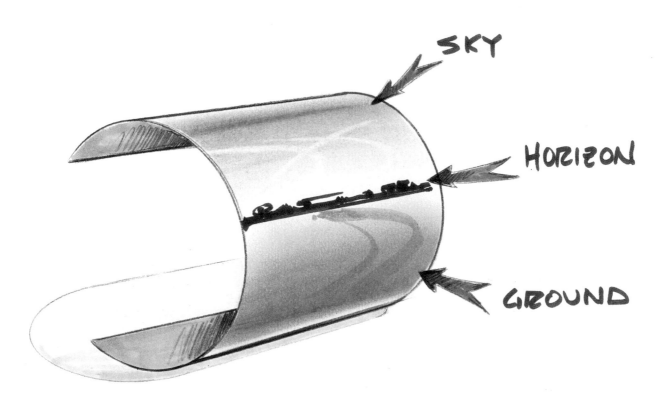

SKY

HORIZON

GROUND

▲ A gradually curved surface will pick up the "perfect" sky, horizon, and ground setup like this. But we usually aren't reflecting a perfect world. There are a lot of objects and obstacles that normally get in the way, so we are used to seeing reflections differently than this example. But this perfect setting makes for a more believable scene reflecting into your bike.

For our tubing examples, number one represents a simplified example of what would be reflected onto a slightly dulled or less reflective finish. Number two takes that same tube, in the same color, and gives us a sample of a much more highly reflective finish. The reflections now have more contrast, and the horizon becomes slightly more detailed. Number three represents a chromed tube. Chrome is much more like a mirror—there is no color tint, so the colors reflected into the chrome tube are much more like they really are. Since our drawings will tend to be done on paper slightly larger than this page, these tubing reflections become a few simple indicated lines.

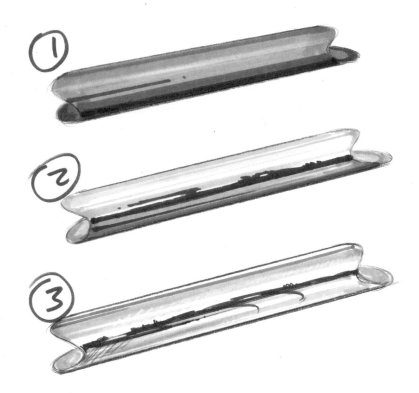

sketch. The use of thumbnails is great for several other situations: helping with proportions, placement on a page, backgrounds, and color selections, to name a few. Don't be embarrassed by the need for a thumbnail sketch. There are many examples in this book of really cool art that is accompanied by its original thumbnail. Most good art utilizes preliminary drawings before a brush is ever put to canvas, or pencil to paper, for a finished sketch.

Since a chopper's gas tank is the largest object with reflections, we'll take a closer look. Though this is the more stylized custom tank, a peanut tank—or some of the other aftermarket tanks available—will exhibit similar characteristics. The dark horizon running through the belly of the tank, lengthwise, is the most prominent reflection. A gradating sky tone "puddles" the color in the middle of the area between the horizon and the outer portions of the tank. The area below the horizon basically does the same thing, but in a warmer tone. Also, there may be a background reflection at the back edges of the upper tank, and the back edges of the bottom portions of the tank may be reflecting ground closest to the tank.

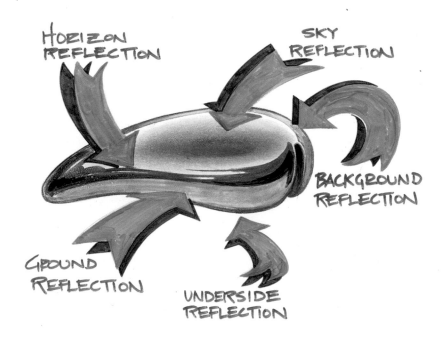

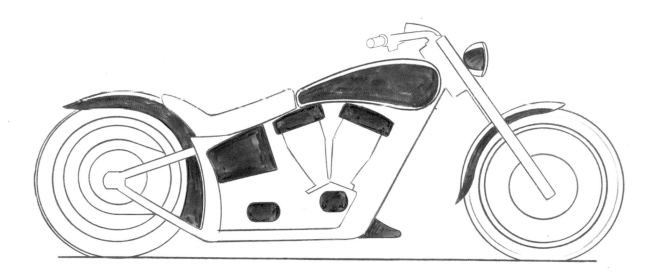

▲  This side view highlights the portions of the chopper that reflect back to the viewer. The red areas represent the body color—painted surfaces reflecting that "perfect" environment. The black areas represent chrome surfaces that face the viewer. Let's see what they realistically look like in a sketch.

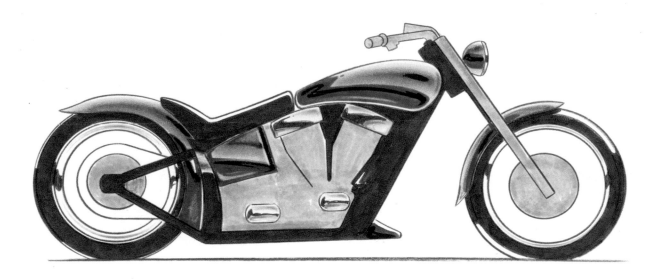

▲  The areas of the bike highlighted in the previous example were rendered in the way we imagine they would look like when reflecting in a simple or "perfect" environment. They reflect the same things: puddle sky tone, horizon, and ground tone. The painted areas are varying values of red. The chrome areas reflect the mirror-like colors of sky, horizon, and ground. Note that the bead portion of the wheels also reflects a chromelike finish.

Another aid to have at your desk is a scale model or toy that can be used to "stage" certain reflection problems before you begin to sketch your master-piece. Although the model won't provide exact solutions to your particular bike's design (unless it is a model of the chopper you are sketching), it will help to show how objects close to the bike may reflect on its surfaces. Be careful though, because a model sitting on your drafting table will not mimic a chopper's real environment.

There are some fairly standard rules to follow in order to give a proper shadow indication. These simple objects give a general idea of how shadows are created. Since choppers exist outside, the light source will always be the sun. Because it is so far out in the distance, the sun's rays are not radiating but rather are essentially parallel, which makes for easier plotting. A shadow is created when the outermost surfaces or edges of the bike that catch the sun's light are cast against another surface, usually the ground.

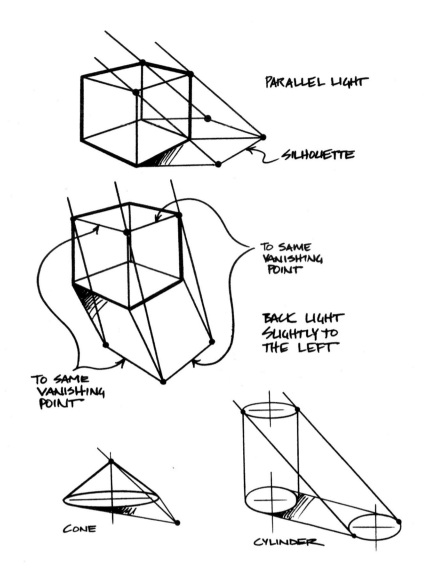

PARALLEL LIGHT

SILHOUETTE

TO SAME VANISHING POINT

BACK LIGHT SLIGHTLY TO THE LEFT

TO SAME VANISHING POINT

CONE

CYLINDER

Although we will be dealing with natural sunlight, this is the effect of artificial light on an object. Unlike the sun, the light rays are radial instead of parallel.

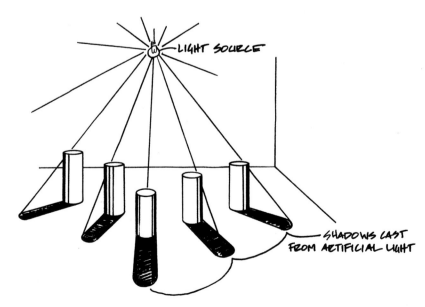

LIGHT SOURCE

SHADOWS CAST FROM ARTIFICIAL LIGHT

64

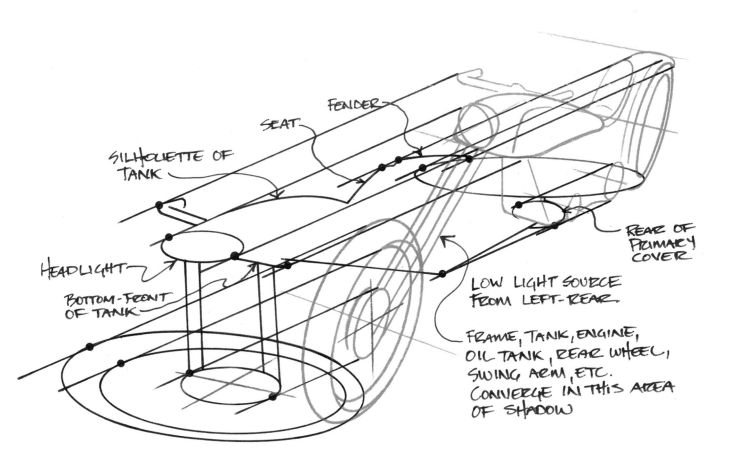

Since shadows can be complicated and mechanical means of plotting are too time consuming, we draw them by observation. However, this diagram shows how one might go about determining where to place shadows. Where possible, I have indicated changing surfaces or corners with a dot. Notice how tires cast an almost perfect ellipse, whose major axis is parallel to the source of the light. Study this to give you a basis for determining shadow problems with your own setups.

You will want to show your subject in the best way, and it may be by placing it in the "perfect" environment, meaning that you may actually create a setting that is unreal. If your bike has a unique feature that you want to show to its best effect, you may render the chopper in a special way to highlight this. It may mean running a reflection through that portion of the bike to help that feature pop out, lighting the bike in such a way so that it draws the eye to this area, or possibly bringing it out with color by adding a warmer tone through it.

Usually, you will not want to copy the reflection detail for detail, but rather "stylize" your reflections to keep them simple. You don't want your reflections to overpower the sketch. Instead, they should blend in and enhance the subject. Fussy, involved reflections may show your ability to copy what happens in the real world, but they don't make for a flashy, punchy drawing. Keep your reflections clean, and your sketch will be, too.

Many of these suggestions for reflections apply for shadows as well. You don't want them overpowering the sketch or looking like they were pasted onto the surface of the chopper. Like reflections, shadows need to follow contours and surface changes. As for ground shadows, they need to be plotted properly so that they

▶ Since I have told you that backlighting an object can lead to disaster, I'll show you an example of backlighting that works like magic. Tom Fritz's *Angle of Attack* painting incorporates severe backlighting with the main source right behind the face mask. But because the light source is so low, its effect is to outline the drag bike, helping to separate it from the background and the ground. Even though in reality the bike would probably look a lot darker with much of its detail obscured because of the harsh light, he created the imaginary world in which the bike inhabits, so he chose to give it more detail—as long as it looks real. Remember, it may not be *true,* but if it looks *real*, then you've done a good job.

help define the bottom of the bike, including its tires. This will give it a foundation off which the bike can play.

I like to do the ground shadow in solid black or a very dark warm color, but it is also cool to sometimes tint the shadow with color to help make the drawing dazzle. You must keep in mind that certain shadows will give the impression that the chopper is floating over a big black hole, ready to fall in at any second. This becomes an extension of what we'll learn in Chapter Seven concerning light sources. Defining the tire's shadow and where the shadow cuts in to separate the components of the bike gives detail and breaks up the shadow's edge. And in doing so, it helps avoid the dreaded black-hole syndrome.

This pen and ink sketch by Keith Weesner shows the importance of a shadow to help ground objects. Keith has made sure that the black background doesn't eliminate those shadows by stippling it away from them. A well-defined shadow really helps to give the drawing some realism.

# *Technique*

Technique means the way you actually draw, as well as the medium or utensil used to achieve the drawing. Everyone has a technique lurking inside them. Your technique is your unique combination of seeing things, your dexterity, a heavy or light touch, ability, experience, and even how you feel on a particular day. These, blended with more mechanical circumstances—such as what type of pencil or marker you use, the type of paper, and whether you choose to draw in color or black and white—make for the characteristics that define your technique.

Just because you cannot do a drawing exactly like some examples shown in this book does not mean you aren't drawing properly. It just may be your technique starting to show itself. That's great! The difference is what makes your own efforts prized and marketable, instead of just copies of someone else's work.

▶ First, let's go back a couple of chapters and see what technical aspects this sketch uses. This diagram shows how light is cast on our theoretical one-, two-, three-box object. The light source will be next to your (the viewer's) ear so that the long side of this 3/4 view is our No. 2 side, the front and top of the bike are the No. 1 side, and the areas pointing away from our light source are its No. 3 side.

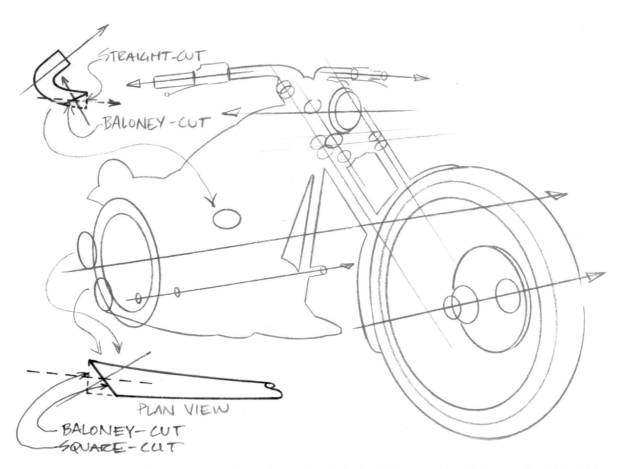

STRAIGHT-CUT

BALONEY-CUT

PLAN VIEW

BALONEY-CUT

SQUARE-CUT

▲   This will be a little hard to follow, because we have so many tubes and circular objects we need to put into perspective, but try to follow along. The outline of the bike is blue (you knew that!), and the red ellipses indicate ends of tubing, foot pegs, grips, and circular objects like tires and the headlight. The straight lines indicate minor axes. It gets a little confusing to diagram the neck area of the bike, with the neck, dog-bone trees, headlight, and forks. Where we have to deviate from our normal major/minor axes and ellipse formula is with the carburetor inlet and exhaust. In both cases, the end-cut of the tube is at an angle, or "baloney slice." We need to indicate the angled cut, so even though there is a major and minor axis, the ellipse we need to use is of a smaller degree for the exhaust (because the cut faces away from us). For this carb outlet, the ellipse indicated is fatter than a circle because the slice is almost square to our view. Got that? The small black and red diagrams try to help you understand this illusion. Once you see it in the finished drawing, I think that you will get it.

I've gathered art from some of the top automobile designers and artists to illustrate the great diversity in techniques that are possible. Even when similar materials are used for some of the drawings, scrutinize how the differences come through. This is one reason someone wants an Ed Newton sketch instead of a Thom Taylor, or why someone would prefer a cartoon from Dave Bell instead of Lance Sorchik. It's technique, the way one draws, that attracts a following or creates interest in that particular person's work.

You may want to try some different styles of drawing yourself, and you definitely should try some different media to see what feels and what looks right to you. While you may discover that you prefer the work of a particular artist, strive for your own technique. Hopefully, along the way you'll achieve a style that is uniquely yours.

Let's incorporate what we know so far and try rendering a custom chopper. See if you understand our setup, and then watch as we render up this dude. This is my bread-and-butter technique—the ol' chalk and marker sketch. I learned it in school and like it because it is fast and because most of my clients need to see things fairly tight.

▶  Once I have roughed out the basic drawing, I trace it more tightly, in this case on bond paper. The painted surfaces are drawn with colored pencil and the rest in black. You may choose to sketch the whole thing in black, which is okay. I have left a little detail out of our Evo-type engine because I'm hoping I can get away with not sketching in all of the details and components. Notice that in a few cases I have indicated reflections of nearby components, like on the front wheel, under the pegs, and on the rear fender next to my swoopy sissy bar.

▲  This is where we start to block in our main colors with marker. The bike is copper, or burnt orange, so those are easy to figure out. I'm going to use a periwinkle for some of the shadows to help push them away from shadows that are closer to our view. A medium gray is used for the front tire, the No. 3 areas of chrome, and the sides turned away from our light source. I have also decided to block in the horizontal graphics on the tank, but have left off part of the black because it needs to gradate up as it turns toward our light source. I snuck in some reflections in the headlight, too.

70

▲   The copper is cleaned up with colored pencil. Then a darker value bronze-type color is introduced where the color turns away from our light source, or where an object or component is close to a painted part—like the air foil. I have left some of the color off of it as well, like the top of the rear fender, because they are pointing up toward our light source and thus need a gradation of chalk. I have blackened in the areas that I chose to go dark, but stopped using straight black about halfway along the bike, because as we go back things get lighter in color, remember? I have layered some darker values into the front tire. I'll blend those colors toward the end of the sketch. The shadows are getting darker, but, again, I cool it as I get farther back on the bike. I'm starting to indicate some reflections in the rocker boxes, exhaust pipes, headlight, trees, and wheels. I keep them as simple as possible—more like stylized reflections than literal ones.

◀   Once we finish the last stage, we almost have real-looking chrome. The missing ingredients are sky tone for surfaces facing up and ground tone for those facing down. These colors should be "puddled in" so that they gradate in all directions of the area you are filling. Sometimes you have to deviate slightly from one component to another to get each part looking like "juicy" chrome, but try to be as consistent as possible. Remember: the sky is up (and blue), and the ground is down (and brown)! Since I had the blue out, I also took care of the graphic lines on the gas tank—the black and white lines gradate up to blue, lighter with the white. And because black is like dark chrome, it reflects everything around it, but in a darker value—in this case a darker blue.

▶ Let's blend some areas. The tires get some black chalk to blend the grays into the black—the tires look more realistic like this. The air foil and rear fender get their gradation of bronze. I also sneak in some blue in the tire to help define it a bit and to help it turn away because cool colors recede. I've detailed a few other parts of the bike like the tank with some white, soft highlights, too.

▲ This is where we get to have fun with paint. Get out a fine brush and start dabbing in some "pigeon highlights" in the hot spots of the rendering. Where the light source would reflect its brightest spot on components, that is where a dab of white gouache should go. Consult the drawings in this book to study where highlights are placed. It should be a little random, but always be consistent with where the light source is. Now, sign your name and get some wind in your face!

▲    Over the last few years John Bell has made the transition from design work—done with the traditional materials such as pencils, markers, and chalk—to painting. These are acrylic paints on wood. John just likes the feel and look of his images on wood. Firstly, he draws what he wants to paint, and then he transfers it to the wood. He does this by chalking the back of the paper sketch and tracing over the lines to transfer the image to the board with the chalk. Then, he's ready to paint.

▲    As long as we're talking about nontraditional ways of drawing choppers, how about One-Shot enamel paint? Dave Bell includes pinstriping in his bag of tricks and will occasionally do a scene with his striping enamels, as he has done on this '37 Chevy glove box door. Gradations are kept to a minimum, which is good for this type of small painting, because too much detail would probably get to busy and it also makes the job easier to do. I count at least 10 to 12 colors!

▲   Tom Fritz sketch done in gouache at under 8 1/2x11 inches. After he was through with his sketch, he used white tape to help frame or crop the painting. By moving the tape around, he can try out different compositions to get the most dramatic look possible. The finished painting appears on pages 66 and 67.

# *Color*

Color enriches a sketch with added interest and dimension. When used effectively, it is an eye-grabbing tool. It draws the eye into the sketch and helps give an added dimension, thanks to a few simple tricks you can try yourself. However, color can just as easily ruin a sketch if overworked or used in the wrong manner.

One thing about choppers is they are usually full of color. Even a black chopper reflects everything around it into that luscious licorice tank and frame. So a lot of the fun in drawing choppers is because of color.

Having a good range of colors available, whether from markers, pencils, or chalks, helps you blend and highlight color with color. If your funds are limited but

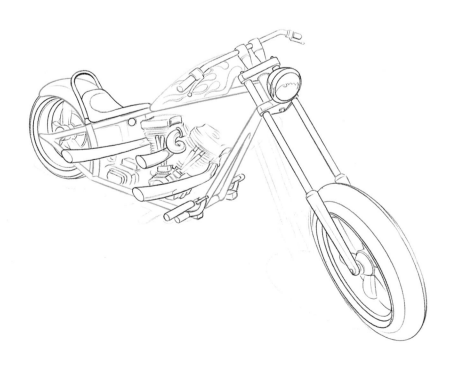

◀ For our classic chopper, this line drawing was traced from a rough underlay on bond paper. There are bond papers available specifically for markers and vellums—such as Vincent vellum—that take chalk and marker very well. This stage could have been done in black pencil, but I like to draw my guidelines in a color close to the final color I will use. If you do use a color, make sure that parts like the pipes, engine, tires, and wheels are drawn in black. You don't want a colored line running around every component of the bike. You may also want to consider keeping your line work on the lighter side so that you can come back in at a later time and punch up what you wish, or leave the lighter lines to almost disappear. Since I knew where this drawing was going, I chiseled them in. Also notice that I plan on having flames on the tank, so I have gone ahead and outlined them as well. And finally, I want to keep my shadow in the light purple/blue range to help push it back and also to give a little bit of contrasting color for the rest of the bike to pop off of. It may not be realistic, but it won't look strange once the drawing is done.

▲ Let's dump some color into this dude. First I fill in the larger areas with the base color for that area. Our bike will be a hot green, so that is what I plug into the frame, gas tank, oil tank, and rear fender. I drop black into the obvious portions of the tire and seat. The portions of these two components that face the light source are left alone to add a lighter value at the next stage. Also, the exhaust and carb inlet will be black, but because the rear tire is in the distance of our perspective space, I don't want it colored in with a dark, harsh color. Instead, I choose a mid-range gray. I also shade the bottom portion of chrome components, and sneak in some minor reflections on the headlight, exhaust, and engine. I fill in the flames with the lightest color that will be used in them, and I reflect a little bit of sky into some of the chrome. Keep your marker strokes random-looking, even if you plot them out to a fine degree. Random does not mean sloppy. Hacked or scribbled marker strokes are distracting and look really amateur. At this stage the drawing looks a bit weak, but we have just begun. We'll punch this up soon enough!

you're itching to try color in your drawings, start with a range of colored pencils or markers within a particular color family. Building up, or "layering," your drawings works better with a range of one or two color families. If you pick a red, consider a lighter, darker, warmer, and cooler version of that red. That will give you a range of four different colors to go with the original red, for a total of five. Having a good range of one color is better than a beginners' set consisting of a green, a blue, a red, etc. Then, if you are feeling like you want to break out from the reds, you can begin to get into other ranges of color and gradually fill out your pallet.

You'll need a few other colors besides your one family of red colors: consider a light blue for sky tones, a warm brown or dirty orange for ground tones, and a black, a white, and a small range of grays to use for chrome and possibly shadows. At this point, all of your choppers will be red, but if you really get into it, you won't care because you'll be rendering some cool bikes.

When it comes to color, there are theories on it, like the classic Munsell and Ostwald color systems (used in most art schools), and techniques to incorporate,

▲   Now we start to bounce the chopper off of the page. Starting at the back, the portions of the tire that are in shade have been darkened, and I have started to put in the wheel reflections. A darker green has been drawn into all of the frame tubing to give it some dimension. By darkening up the bottom of the tubing, it is starting to look round instead of flat. That darker green has been added as a secondary reflection into the rear fender, and also the oil tank, gas tank, and neck. The seat has been detailed with a dark gray marker, and then blended with a black pencil. I have darkened the areas around the engine to help punch it out and have started to refine the chrome reflections in the chrome tubing. The horizon reflection has been added to the headlight bulb, and I have layered in darker grays on the front tire. These will be blended in the next step. I have also decided to help punch the engine out from the shadow a little more by putting a fine gray outline around it. This is not realistic, but it won't be distracting. It is one of those things you can do once you know what is and isn't possible.

like tinting, contrasting colors, complementary colors, and so on. But in drawing a chopper, we are dealing not so much with systems or theories as we are trying to depict a motorcycle in a particular color. While it's not as simple as it sounds, it *is* fairly easy to master. So let's concentrate on chopper color theory and leave the other information for another time and another book, perhaps one specifically on color at your local library, if you are interested.

Cool colors such as blue, purple, or green tend to recede or go back into a perspective sketch. Conversely, warm colors such as yellow, orange, and red come forward in a sketch. So even for a hot-yellow bike, you might consider tinting the yellow in a soft, cool color toward its tail, so that this portion of the bike moves away from the viewer. As the bike comes closer to the viewer in perspective, really let the yellow scream at the front portion of the chopper. It helps set the bike into the perspective space of your paper.

Another trick with color, as we have mentioned earlier, is that as you go back into the perspective space, you will also want to make the chopper lighter

▲ This may look done, but it still has a way to go. This is mainly the "bring out the chrome" part of drawing. The core of the chrome tubing reflects up to the sky, hence the sky tone. Some of the chrome reflects components that are right next to it, so that is why you may see some green or dark gray indicated on the chrome. There may also be some shadow indicated on the tubing, like the portions of the frame just below each exhaust pipe. I put in the light value of green that reflects the sky on the rear fender and oil tank. The trees, headlight, rocker boxes, and wheels all get the chrome treatment. The surfaces of the wheels that face up get blue; the surfaces facing down get the earth tone. The same goes for the pegs, headlight bulb, and everything else you want to look like chrome. Only puddle the blue into the areas you wish to reflect the sky. If the whole area gets plugged in with blue, it will not look like chrome, so leave some white around your sky reflections. The front tire is detailed, and I put in the tread and highlight the tread based on what edges are facing our light source. Also note that the tire is reflected in the side of the down fork. And finally, I detail the flames on the tank. Since the handle grip is in front of the tank, and there are flames interrupting the side of the tank, I choose not to run a horizon line through the tank—even though it would be the correct thing to do. There is just too much going on to add another "thing" to the tank. That's called "artist's prerogative" in "Thom's Book of Rules"! Let's put some finishing touches on this and then take a ride down PCH!

in value. These changes in color should be very subtle and used more as a veiled trick than as something overt. If the change is too obvious, it becomes distracting and you lose the effect you are trying to achieve. It may even give the illusion that the bike is painted in a blend of one color into another. Once you master the use of color, this might be a fun experiment to try. But for now, let's concentrate on a single color.

Here's another trick to use with color: since the chopper is almost always viewed outdoors, the sky reflects a subtle blue cast over the surfaces of the bike that point up. But don't forget that those surfaces pointing up also get lighter, as in the one-, two-, three-box examples. And just as the sky reflects from above, the ground reflects into the lower portions of the chopper's components. These ground reflections will cast a warm yellow/brown tone into those lower surfaces.

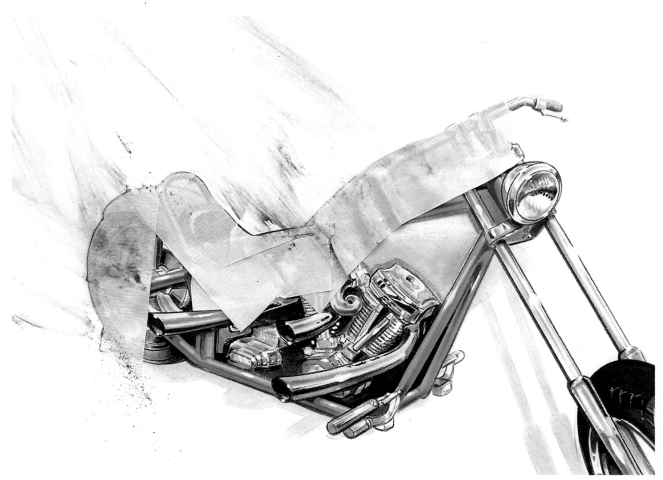

▲ Since the drawing is almost done, let's put in the background. To start, I tape off the upper portions of the bike to protect it from the color soup we'll be sloshing behind it. Don't forget to use drafting tape or Frisket film, otherwise you'll be ripping up part of your chopper when you pull off any tape that is very sticky. Once the tape is down, I scratch an X-ACTO blade against blue and purple pieces of chalk to get the dust onto the background. I choose colors that complement the shadow and contrast slightly with the green, and thus get some extra punch from the green. I squirt some Bestine solvent onto a tissue, and in long, light strokes I wash into the paper the combination of Bestine and chalk dust with the juicy tissue. Keep it random and leave some paper coming through. Practice until you are comfortable trying this, otherwise you may ruin the drawing you have spent hours or even days on. Let it dry for a few minutes and finish up with some pigeon highlights.

With the cooler sky tones in the upper surfaces and the warm ground tones in the lower portions of the bike, your rendering will start to take on some real-world characteristics. As you start thinking about the use of warm and cool tones, try experimenting with how far you want to go to introduce these cast tones into your drawing. Too little and you hardly notice, while too much lends a strange "circus wagon" look to your drawing.

There is another pit to avoid falling into when applying color to your drawing: if you are too timid with your colors, you can give the illusion that the bike is made of tinted glass. The drawing takes on a characteristic of being visually lighter than air. So when you lay in color, try to remember to keep "volume" in the drawing. The bike is a very heavy, solid object (even if things do occasionally rattle loose from that V-twin vibration). You want it to have that firm appearance in your drawing. If the chopper is a light color to begin with, the variation in value will be less. The No. 1 side of your imaginary box may be only slightly lighter than your No. 2 side. I know this is a lot to remember, so try these suggestions one at a time, and keep referring back to this and other chapters for these useful tips.

▲   What are pigeon highlights? They are the little white hot spots that make a rendering dazzle and sparkle. Don't be timid. Get out your white gouache and make sure it is slightly soupier than pancake batter. Then stick your Series 7 Windsor Newton brush into the soup, and start dabbing away in every portion of the chopper you think needs that extra sparkle. Obviously, the portion of the rims directly opposite of your light source needs a couple of dabs, and anything else you think will be reflecting the sun, for that is what these hot spots represent. I have even swiped a little white onto the black leather seat and the front tire and its tread, just to give them a little more contrast. When you can logically get surfaces to go light, dark, light, dark, it adds extra interest for the viewer. I have indicated a few more flutes in the glass cover for the headlight. Once you're done, sign it, blow some fixative on it so that it won't smear, and you're ready to get your face blown riding down the road on your latest chopper. Just don't get a ticket!

▲ Once you become comfortable with color and how it's used, you can go completely against everything you know and try some different things. My contemporary Indian board tracker isn't at all based in reality when it comes to the colors I have chosen—but it is an interesting and fun experiment in the use of colors.

▲ Color says it all in this Ed Newton sketch. Although the background drawings explain most of the bike's design details, the side-view color sketch really makes you take notice. Imagine if this were all done with the blues used in the background. It would not have nearly the punch and interest that Newton's choice of colors lends to the drawing. When doing this blended paint job in sketch form, Ed had to gradually blend the colors while being very careful not to represent the bike's color as some harsh red light shining on the back of a yellow custom.

82

I have included this Keith Weesner painting to illustrate that you can still create a believable painting without using a wide range of colors. Keith kept his color pallet limited to oranges and browns, with just a little bit of green on the primary cover to give an indication of sky tone. Note how the metalflake paint on the Trumpet's gas tank is handled. Instead of hot spots, there's a series of small highlights that concentrate and then spread out from their core. A darker outline gradually appearing around the tank indicates the flakes lying on their sides and creating somewhat of a shadow in the paint.

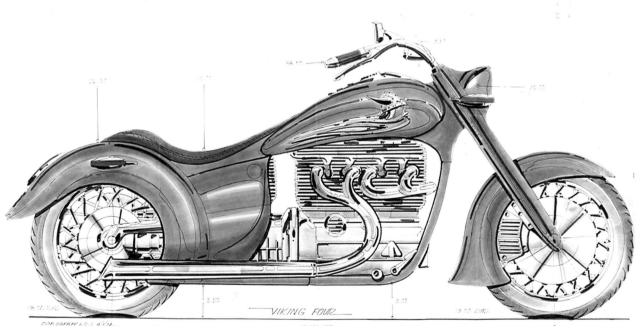

VIKING FOUR

▲ This Don Varner sketch for Bob Dron, owner of Oakland Harley-Davidson, makes a point about marker sketches. Don's sketch was done with a combination of really juicy and really dry markers. You have to know when to use which one. The wet markers give you the nice blended look on the painted surfaces. The dry markers give a subtle, single-color gradation for the chrome and tires. Don't use dry markers for painted surfaces—they tend to get scratchy and uneven. In addition, blending two or three colors with dry markers ends up looking overworked and basically a real mess. And don't use wet markers for gradations in small areas, like chrome components and thin tires; there just isn't enough real estate to get a good blend in such small spaces. By the way, this is a restyle version of a Viking inline four-cylinder motorcycle built in Sweden.

# *Presentation*

Y ou've just knocked out a screaming sketch of a vintage Fat Bob, but you need some way to enhance it rather than just letting it stand alone. This can be as simple as adding a background or border, or as elaborate as positioning it on a hill with 20 other choppers above the night lights of Los Angeles. There are a million and one ways to come up with techniques or secondary objects to enhance your chopper sketch, so we will only scrape the surface of possibilities in this book.

▶ Tom Fritz's painting *Hard Chargin'* incorporates a very dramatic placement of the bikes and riders in the one-point perspective layout. You can see, hear, and smell the action in this presentation. Note that as the objects go farther back into the painting, they use lighter values. Also, there is actually a relatively limited color pallet, yet we don't feel cheated. Although the one-point perspective is thought to be a more simplistic way to draw in perspective, you can see that when it's done with a strong layout of the elements, it becomes very powerful.

I like to just swish some color into the background as an abstract backdrop to the subject. It is quick and simple—just the way I like it. But I have noticed that some artists who do this type of background slop it around to the extent that it looks like it's swallowing up the bike. Or, it's so messy that you can't keep your eyes off of it—sort of like a bad car accident. Keep the backgrounds light and the abstract shapes simple and clean, not choppy and scribbled. You want it to look like the same dude did them both. When you spend all that time sketching a cool bike, it's a shame to blow it with a bad background.

This is a really punchy rendering by Ed Newton. He sketched the bike and added some reflections with a marker, and then he scanned the whole thing into his computer to plug in the rest of the color. Besides being a cool design, it has a really dynamic presentation, incorporating the demon in the background and also a hint of the demon in the shadow. The green background contrasts with the red, which makes the red more brilliant. Cantilevering the engine out there would be one cool trick to pull off. What a wild bike this would be in reality!

# Archfiend

# Cartoons

V irtually every time you freehand-sketch a chopper, you have created a cartoon. Why? Because you have exaggerated the bike, or drawn it slightly out of proportion—even if you didn't intend to do this. Stretching, squishing, leaning, and tilting—the more of these that are present in your drawing, the more you remove your sketch from reality. But it sure is fun.

Some find it easier to draw a cartoon of a bike, while others find it a bit more difficult than doing a straightforward sketch. You may find yourself drawn naturally to the latter, and that is fine. For those who wish to enter the zany world of cartoon fun but find it a bit hard to grasp, you may want to first concentrate on drawing a chopper as well as you can. Once you reach a certain comfort level, you can ease into the cartoon world. By taking your ability to draw well-proportioned sketches and then exaggerating them a bit, you can explore the changes in the relationships of elements that make up a cool bike sketch. Kicking the front end way out is one of the easiest proportion changes you can make to a bike sketch. Exaggerating the sizes of the wheels or tires is another. Frame or engine proportions that are heightened or reduced, elongated or squeezed, can give your drawing any feeling you may want to convey.

Rather than have me blather on, check out the accompanying examples culled from some of the best in the business. Many of these artists have been doing this since the 1960s, so don't be intimidated by the high quality they display.

Study what makes these drawings so special, and practice giving your cartoons that same look. Notice how each of the artists has his own unique style. Strive to come up with a look that is uniquely yours. But most importantly, have fun!

## Dave Bell

Dave's an artist, philosopher, historian, comedian, hot rod personality, and pin-striper, among other things. We'll stick with the art and pinstriping here. Hailing from outside St. Paul, Minnesota, he has lots of time during those long winters to draw in his distinctive style, which he's been doing for four decades. He's mainly an ink slinger, but he does get into color work on occasion. Although he is known for his black-and-white cartoons, when it comes to pinstriping, he is known for wild use of color, incorporating a lot of different colors into a single job.

Dave has been doing his cartoon series *Henry HiRise* in the back of *Street Rodder* magazine for almost the full 35 years of its publication. He starts off with light pencil sketches before going over them with India ink. Many times he will do his one-panel cartoons in a very large format, which then gets reduced to fit in the magazine. I don't know how he is able to get so much content into one cartoon, and then lay it out all together on a single large piece of paper besides! He recently confided to me that he really misses his Triumph chopper, which he sold a few years ago. Sorry, Dave.

## Lance Sorchik

Lance and his wife, Diane, are schoolteachers out of Sussex, New Jersey. Lance is able to distort a car or bike more than anyone I can think of. The reason he can do this is because he has a great handle on perspective, knows proportion, and is very intimate with hot rods and choppers. The deal is, once you know how to draw accurately, you can really start to challenge the rules, which Lance does with gusto! He has been kind enough to include some rough sketches so that you can see how he starts off. His drawings have a lot of expression and movement, which makes them fun to look at.

These line sketches were for the client Pinnacle, who commissioned Lance to come up with a logo. From these three sketches, Pinnacle picked the side view. Note that the drawings have been worked up from faint line work, and then chiseled in and darkened up. You can sort of "feel" your way around by using the faint lines like a road map. There isn't a ton of detail, just enough to get the idea across.

▶ The finished logo done in India ink. There's more detail, and some of the components have changed from the initial sketch. The black flag behind the bike helps to pop it off of the page because the drawing does not have a lot of dark values in it, thus allowing the client to come back to Lance at a later date and have colors added.

Custom Cycles

"Beyond Badass!"

Another side view that displays a different character than the last drawing. Once Lance has a rough to go by, he inks in the final drawing. When he is completed, he scans it into his computer and colors it in with Photoshop. The color gradations are fairly simple and broad, but that's okay because he has a lot of detail in the line drawing. You don't need to get really involved with reflections and color details. The line work helps to delineate the drawing.

## Keith Weesner

The "Weez" has developed a very clean style of drawing and painting. He has worked on and off for Warner Bros. animation for years and is now concentrating on doing art pieces for a living. Elsewhere in this book are some of his paintings, but we'll concentrate on his cartoon work here. Keith loves vintage stuff, which really comes out in his drawings. One unique thing I see him doing is blacking out an area in his drawing, then coming in with white gouache to peck at the details. This is a lot easier than figuring out the details and then trying to fill in the negative areas. It's not cheating, it's just easier, which is why cartoons can be fun. There are no rules, so go for what feels good to you!

▲ Interestingly, there is not a lot of line work in this cartoon. The areas that exhibit detail were put in with white gouache. Keith has a lot of areas blocked in with black, which makes for a very bold cartoon against the white background. Also note that there are no wheel spokes, yet the drawing reads well without them. Nice and simple.

▶ This would be a great panel for a sequence cartoon. By using a side view, Keith is able to backlight the bike so you see the outline of the engine and components. Even though there are no drawn-in details, you can use your imagination to see the entire bike because he has done such a good job of presenting it to the viewer. With the position of the chopper and the Maltese cross swinging in the air, there is a lot of action, too.

Keith's idea for a mad motorcycle monster started with this pencil drawing. As with some of the other rough sketches you have seen, light line work helps to pave the way for heavier lines once you know the way to go. Details are almost scribbled in, which is fine at this stage. Compare the first version to the second. Note the design differences with the helmet, peanut tank, arm, and direction of the front wheel. Keith wanted to try other things in his cartoon, so why not?

## Thom Taylor

Because I'm mostly involved with real-world design assignments, I find that cartoons are a breath of fresh air, and I really enjoy doing them. You don't have to concern yourself with exacting proportions or finite details, and you are really creating in an imaginary world. I exaggerate different aspects of the bike for each drawing I do, so it is hard to say exactly what my "formula" is. Shown are a number of different styles and media so you can see some of the ways I work.

Thom 7.97 ©

*Cadaclism* is this imaginary '59 Cadillac-type bike. Since it is a Cadillac, it *has* to be pink! This view was chosen to emphasize the rear of the bike, which is the focal point with the fins and all. Note that the taillights, which stick way out from the fins, are not only reflected into the chrome trim right below the red lens, but also farther down on the chrome pod. That chrome is a mirror, so you always need to be thinking about what will be reflected into it. This sketch was done in chalk and marker.

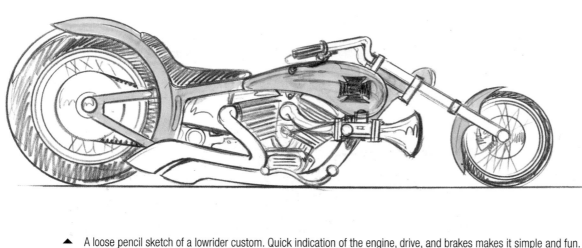

▲ A loose pencil sketch of a lowrider custom. Quick indication of the engine, drive, and brakes makes it simple and fun. This is an idea sketch for a line of toys. At this "thinking" stage, the yellow was thrown in to show the client what components would be painted and which would be chromed plastic. This is all freehand with the exception of the wheels and tires.

▶ Pen and ink—or at least that is how this looks. Actually, I hate using India ink because I'm such a klutz that I always smear it around and make a mess. So to fake it, I use fine-tip markers. They dry instantly and give an almost ink-like line. Since I do such heavy line work anyway, I tend to not get into the fine lines that an ink pen can give. The wheel and fork are actually out of perspective in relation to one another, but I did this so that you could see more of the wheel and fork—in other words, so your brain reads more. Once you know the perspective basics, you can break the rules to fit different situations.

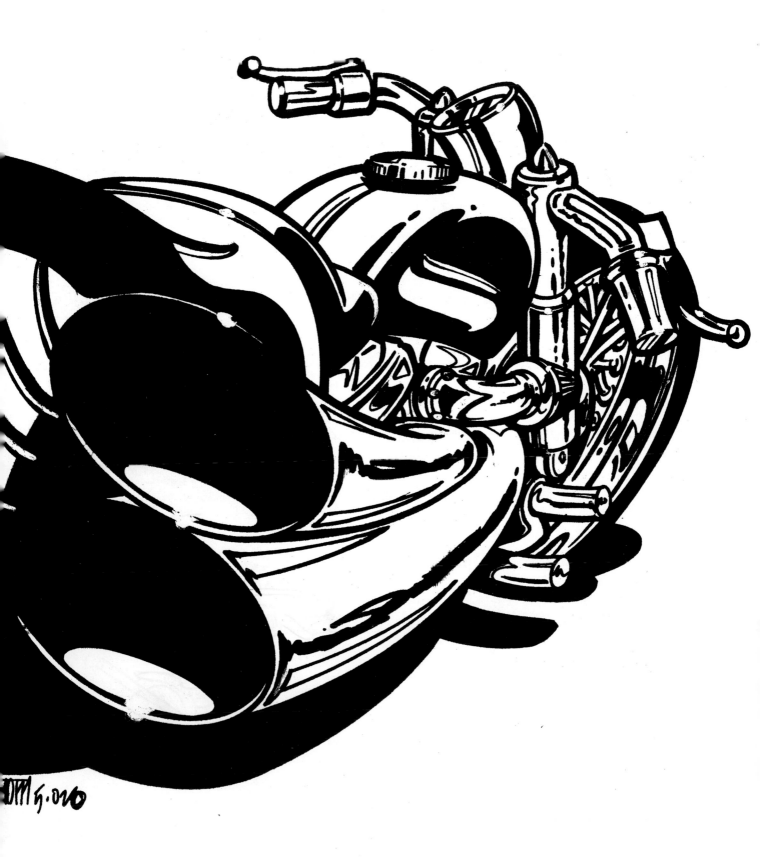

▶ A more finished sketch of the V-Rod for a potential toy line. The rake, exhaust, and rear wheel are greatly exaggerated, and the framework and other details are beefed up. I try to play light tones against dark so that the drawing gets really contrast-y. Is that a word? No chalk here, just marker and pencil.

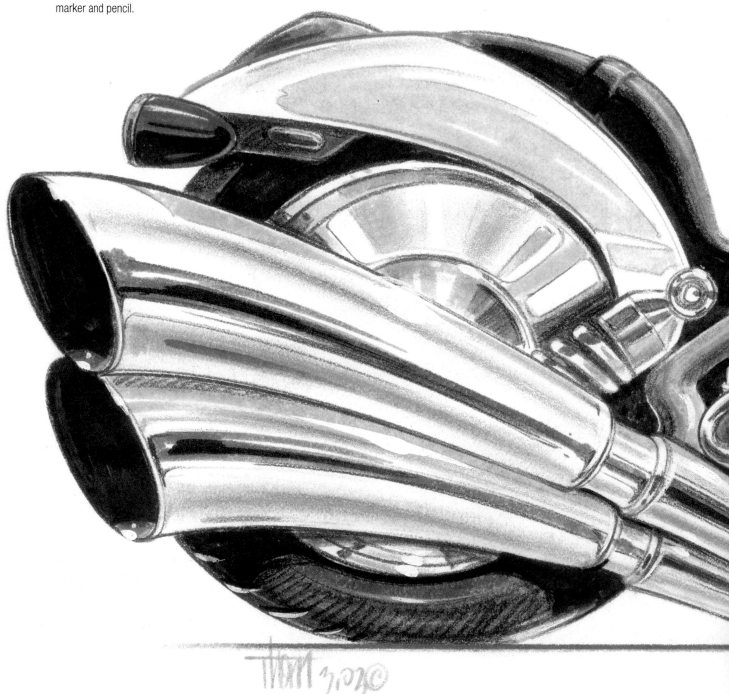

► Another quick pencil sketch of an old cantilever Indian. The client never saw this one, which explains the lack of detail and very loose line work. This was done for me, just to get it from my head to paper. No templates here—just loose, fun sketching!

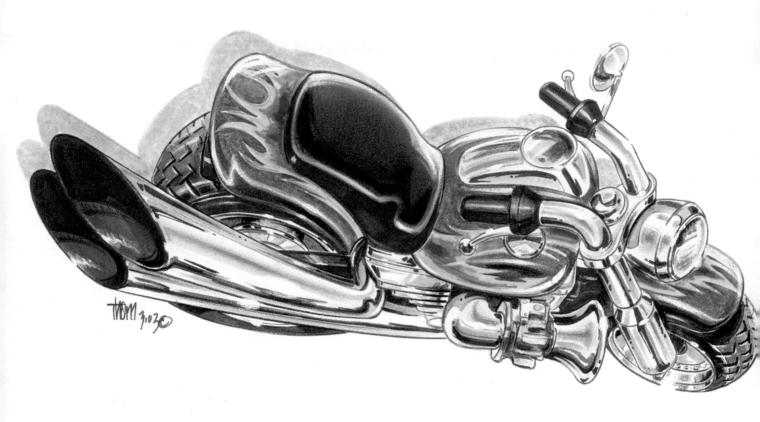

▲   In this chalk and marker sketch, I came back in with white gouache to help separate some of the surfaces of the fenders and tank, as well as to help them go into the distance visually. Lightening up the surfaces farthest away from the viewer helps the object go back into the perspective space you have created. Remember that trick? Again, this was done with colored marker and chalk.

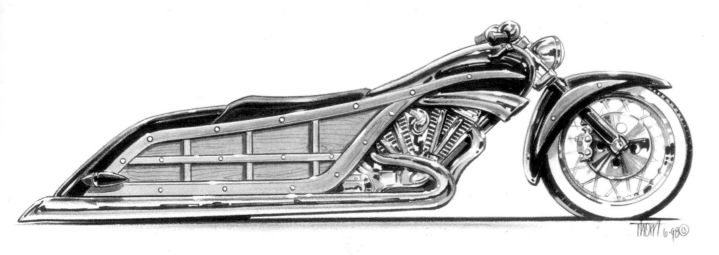

▲   Although this looks fairly real, the front tire/wheel and low back end indicate that it is not. The "woody bike" was rendered entirely in marker and pencil, except for the magenta gradations in the tank and fenders. This was a bit difficult to do, as the original drawing was on 8 1/2x11-inch paper.

## Darrell Mayabb

Darrell's drawings are on the border of being more realistic and less cartoony, but when you stop to scope out the proportions of the bikes and compare different components to one another, you can see that they fit into the cartoon world. One thing that is common with almost all of Darrell's drawings is that he is not shy about throwing in a lot of color, which is a lot of fun for him and makes his sketches fun to look at. Darrell is a master of many disciplines, including fine art and photography. All of these cartoons have been done exclusively on the computer.

A very "design-y" bike with complete bodywork. Note that the exhaust becomes part of the bike's design. Also note that Darrell laid in a contrasting color for the background not only to impart movement, but also to help pop the sketch off the page. When doing this, you have to make sure that if the background is a darker value, then add a lighter value to help separate the object from the background, and vice versa. Darrell was kind enough to include the line drawings he started with—which he created completely on the computer.

© 2000

Another wild design from Darrell, this time with a "steel-y" finish. He has given it this look by running parallel stripes of color through the panels, but not parallel to the ground like a reflection. And the highlights are "chattered" as opposed to hard, crisp lines or hot spots. Again, the background helps to give movement and to pop off the bike, which is a lighter value playing against the darker background. Note some of the subtle design changes from the line sketch to the finished piece.

© 2000

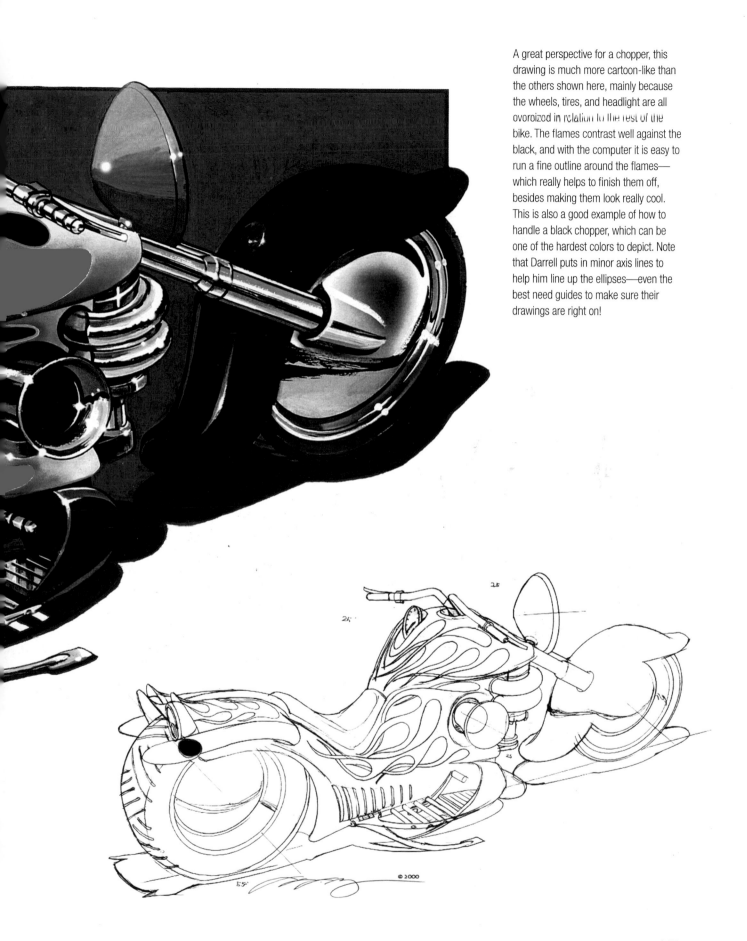

A great perspective for a chopper, this drawing is much more cartoon-like than the others shown here, mainly because the wheels, tires, and headlight are all oversized in relation to the rest of the bike. The flames contrast well against the black, and with the computer it is easy to run a fine outline around the flames—which really helps to finish them off, besides making them look really cool. This is also a good example of how to handle a black chopper, which can be one of the hardest colors to depict. Note that Darrell puts in minor axis lines to help him line up the ellipses—even the best need guides to make sure their drawings are right on!

## Dave "Big" Deal

Dave Deal is our pope of cartoons—not the first, but definitely one of the car and bike cartoon pioneers. So much so, in fact, that Disney asked him to help develop the look for the vehicles designed for the animated Pixar movie *Cars*. After all of these years he still loves to draw, but the computer has taken over the coloring aspect of his work. He was kind enough to include some preliminary sketches and actually created a couple of new pieces just for this book! Here he explains his progression in his own words.

▶ This was the first idea sketch, done in a restaurant on the place mat. Could be on a napkin, or envelope, or whatever. I shoot it digitally and enlarge it, then print it and use it as a basis for my first tracing, which follows. This is the best way to carry spontaneity of the sketch through to the final art.

▶ Here, I traced a print of the place mat sketch, making some refinements. It is fairly stiff and not exactly what I wanted, so, more tracing paper.

◀ This is a tracing of the first tracing, which has refined the details a bit more. Tracing paper is important because it allows you to see through and not lose your original sketch idea.

◀ Here, I begin in earnest. This drawing is a tracing of the previous tracings and is done with more attention to line quality. I use Prismacolor 935 Black pencils because they tend to smear less and have a full range of value, from very light to very dense. They reproduce exactly as they appear to the eye.

COVER,

CALIPER

▲ More details are added, bit by bit. Line quality is maintained.

▶ Some values and shadow contrasts are added with more line work. I work all over the drawing to keep from getting bogged down with any one area.

◀ Almost finished with the pencil work, now, I go back and "noodle" in shading and reflections, making more "arty" looking shapes and lines as I proceed.

▲ When the drawing is finished, I turn the tracing paper over and work in values and contrasts with AD markers, darkening rubber and shadows with a #5 warm marker and chrome reflections with a #3. I have used this technique for more than 30 years, and although others may do the same thing, I "invented" it for myself way back when. I also work in the flesh values with the help of a blender marker. It lightens the other values and softens the edges.

▲   Now, I scan or photograph the art with a digital camera and it's into the Mac G4 for color rendering. Adobe Photoshop is where I do my airbrushing now. It's a lot cleaner than the old way. Always use the "Layers" function to airbrush. Do not "Flatten" the image until you are sure the layer is exactly what you want. Also, it is advisable to use the "Multiply" setting on the layer so it will not destroy the underlying line art.

▶   For the purists, I have mixed some themes here—"old school" with "new school"—but this is my chopper and I built it the way I wanted. The dude on the chopper is a stereotype of what I think a Harley rider looks like, at least a fairly clean one— not too radical, but he's an "outlaw" to be sure. In the cartoon world, by the way, riders do not have to wear helmets or have license plates. It's a way cool place.

## Ed Newton

Ed has been doing cartoons for over 40 years! He came into prominence when Ed "Big Daddy" Roth employed him exclusively to do all of the great shirt and decal designs he sold throughout the 1960s. Although Roth's name was on the designs, it was Ed Newton actually doing them. Of course he has gone on to greater things, but he still finds time to knock out a cartoon now and then. Today, Ed sketches out the drawing, and then scans it into the computer and colors it in much the same way as Dave Deal does. His earlier 'toons were all done by hand, with India ink for the line work and gouache for color.

Years ago, the model company MPC marketed a plastic scale version of a three-wheeler that Ed Newton designed, based around an old Harley Servicar. Built by Ed "Big Daddy" Roth, it became known as the *Mail Bike.* MPC has been out of business for years, but the kit is being re-released by Retro Hobby Inc. (www.retrohobby.com) with new art, shown here. It's the same ol' Ed, but these days he's putting in the color with his computer's Painter program.

# *People*

After you have gained good knowledge of drawing and rendering a chopper, the best way to take it from being just a bike to something more is by adding people. It does so much; it gives scale to the drawing, it adds interest, it creates a scene—in other words, it helps to show something happening, and more. After all, choppers aren't just static objects—they are meant to carry people, so people can be an integral part of your chopper drawings if you so choose.

▶ Tom Fritz is one of the most exciting artists currently painting cars and bikes. If you can draw yourself away from this fantastic oil painting called *Path Less Traveled*, imagine the vintage Harley as a static painting without the rider. There really would not be any life to it! But with the rider and his relationship to the bike, this becomes a dramatic painting with action. Your mind sees the splashing water and the rider tromping his way through the stream before commencing with his journey. There's something going on—a story—and the person really helps to give that impression.

After attending countless rat rod shows, John Bell began to capture the "look" of some of the women attending these events and incorporate them into his drawings. John creates creatures and settings for movies and video games, so he is well versed in the intricacies of drawing living beings. The relaxed stance combined with the rider's attitude makes the bike almost secondary.

In this chapter you'll find some tips and guides to drawing people, but the best way to actually get a handle on drawing natural-looking people is to observe and then sketch what you see. There are so many nuances to drawing the human body that observation and a critical eye is the only way to really learn how.

Another John Bell sketch that incorporates a natural-looking person to add some realism. Also note the line quality—how John lightly sketches in the main parts first, and then builds up the drawing from there. For a sketch, there is quite a lot of information without a lot of actual detail.

▲  Keith Weesner includes a lot of people in his paintings. We've seen some of the early sketches he does before starting a painting. Just as with the John Bell sketches, the addition of a woman with attitude gives the painting a whole different look. It is also interesting that just a few colors are utilized in this painting—mainly black, maroon, and white, with a little pink and orange for the background. Yet, the painting reads as a complete depiction, even without any other colors.

I have observed through the years that the artists who do the best chopper drawings tend to draw people only so-so. At least that is what I tell myself to satisfy my rather meager attempts at putting people into my drawings. Unfortunately for me, the artists' work in this chapter blows a pretty big hole into that theory! Just as I am always trying to make my "people" better, you should strive to do likewise. I know my drawing weaknesses, which makes me try just a little harder!

In this chapter you'll find some really great examples from illustrators who include people in their drawings day in and day out. Your people drawings won't look like these to start, but that old chant—*practice, practice, practice*—is what it takes to get a natural-looking person to enhance your chopper drawings.

◀ We've shown a Weesner painting with a person. Here's a sketch of a woman riding her Harley into the breeze! The details of the bike are fairly simple, but the woman is chiseled in, which nicely illustrates the contours and details involved in drawing a person.

# Computers

Let's get one thing clear right off the bat: computers will not draw for you. They are only tools to assist you in drawing. A computer may make you better, but only if you have a working knowledge of the previous chapters in this book. I've seen a lot of computer drawings, and you can immediately tell who has a solid understanding of the drawing basics and who has an understanding of the basics of computer programs. Don't delude yourself into thinking otherwise. Everything your computer will do will only aid, not substitute, your ability to draw. With this understanding and some imagination, developing a computer sketch of your favorite chopper can be fun and rewarding.

As a tool, the computer becomes another medium you can use to create your work. Just as a pencil sketch, pastel rendering, or oil painting gives a unique look to your work, so, too, will a computer. In fact, the computer can actually make

▶ Charlie Smith chooses an almost completely enclosed custom bike he designed to show this step-by-step breakdown. He told me that the rendering capabilities of Photoshop are so fine that he has had to back off of the finish of his illustrations because they were becoming almost photo-realistic. He scans a sketch done by hand into Photoshop and does a quick thumbnail with color plugged in it. Once he gets a general road map for where he will place color, he assigns the colors he chooses to the pencil sketch and produces his final piece. All of the marker, airbrush, and final details are done on the computer.

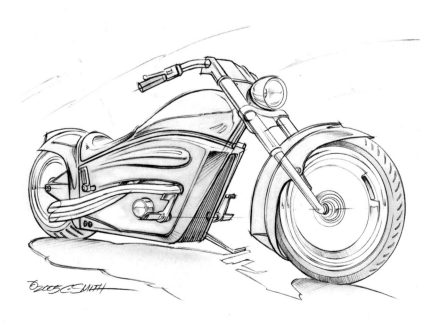

©2005 C.SMITH

© 2005 C Smith

*Top Banana* is a design by Darrell Mayabb that shares some design with Charlie's green bike. He creates the line drawing on computer before transferring it to Photoshop, where he uses the "painter" process. An accomplished artist, he compares Photoshop to an "electronic airbrush." He also does some T-shirt design that requires color separations. In these cases, he uses the Illustrator program because he needs vector art to plug in butted color, which the Photoshop program does not allow.

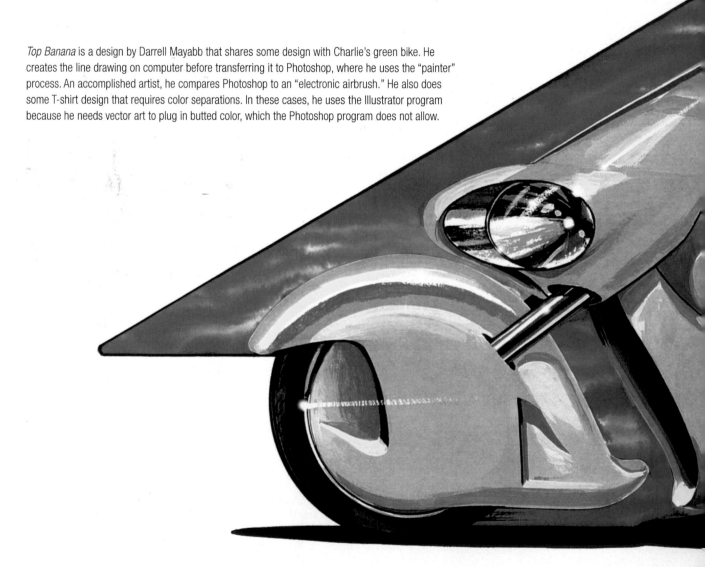

your drawing look like it was pencil, pastel, or oil rendered. It also offers you choices and looks that could never be achieved with real-world tools.

In this chapter I have assembled some really great computer sketches by some really great artists. The common thread running through each of these artists' works is that the artists are all remarkable freehand illustrators. In some cases these examples were completely drawn on the computer, but for most there was some hand sketching incorporated into the art.

© 2000

▲  Jim Bruni sketch started life as an old, damaged photo, which—as he puts it—he "treated with a healthy disrespect" to achieve what you see here. He scanned it into Photoshop, and then threw color around and returned to filter the areas he colored to achieve certain textures, or a "shaggy-ness." Modifying the adaptations performed to the photo took it away from its origins and helped to give this the sketchy look Jim was after.

For most graphics applications, the Macintosh, or Mac, is the gorilla of the industry, but many of these programs are compatible with PC computer systems, too. If you have a computer and want to learn how to use it with your sketches, the best thing to do is to scan your hand-drawing and experiment with the programs most commonly used by illustrators: Photoshop and Illustrator. As many of these artists have pointed out to me, there are possibly hundreds of ways to do the same operation within each of these programs—no two illustrators will attack a drawing the same way. That is why I have chosen not to give step-by-step instructions but, instead, have provided some cool illustrations for you to study.

With your knowledge of drawing by hand, and your imagination enhanced with the capabilities of the computer, you are well into the twenty-first century way of drawing like a pro!

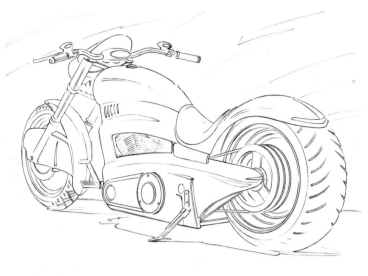

Charlie Smith's *Fade to Black* custom chopper. With these views, he has given the client all of the necessary details to help envision exactly what the bike will look like. Note that we have also included a front-view pencil sketch that helped Charlie define the entire bike before he actually started to draw it from the rear. When designing, you have to be able to imagine all 360 degrees of the product so that no portion is faked.

©2005 C.Smith

# Schools

L et's say that this drawing choppers thing has captured your interest. Let's say you want to try to make it your life's work. Or maybe you want to go to work where you can draw and design motorcycle components. If you're really consumed by it— or have always wanted to dream up the next Harley-Davidson—and you have sustained that interest after reading this book, then a next possible step is to look into enrolling in a professional school that caters to product or automotive design.

Think about it: every product from an iPod to a semi truck needs to be designed. That means it needs to be drawn. There are schools that teach this process and lay a strong career foundation. In the United States there are two colleges, in particular, that have a great reputation for this type of education. Art Center College of Design in Pasadena, California, and College for Creative Studies (CCS) in Detroit, Michigan, are famous for their graduates making up the bulk of designer staffs in the consumer product, toy, and automotive design fields.

Both Art Center and CCS are accredited four-year colleges that provide you with the necessary skills and training to forge a career in product and automotive design, as well as designing for the movie industry. After all, the movie studios need futuristic motorcycles and even whole new worlds. These schools employ working professionals who take the time to teach, so you are instructed by those who are in the field and who probably have degrees from the very school at which they teach. All aspects of design are covered, with an emphasis on conceptual drawing and visualization. I am a graduate of Art Center and have taught there, too, so I'm a firm believer in going this direction if you are really serious about doing this type of work.

Let's face it: most of the companies you would be interested in working for are probably cool companies—which means they appeal to a lot of younger people, including design college graduates. So, why would the company you're dying to work for hire you if they have a choice to hire someone who has graduated with a design degree? Even if you are qualified, it makes sense that the college grad gets the first shot. So, if you want to do this, check out the school of your choice, talk to a counselor, and figure out how you can swing this.

Obviously the downside is the cost—these schools aren't cheap! Grants at the high school level are one avenue to pursue, and student loans have become almost mandatory.

Some state colleges offer product or automotive design curriculums, including Cleveland Institute of Art in Ohio and Wayne State in Detroit. Do your research on all of the schools you have an interest in attending. Keep in mind that some colleges get into the *process* of design without getting into the actual *conceptualization* of a product or car. That's okay, but ask to see completed projects and models. If they show you a notebook of diagrams, research, and a few pictures, look elsewhere. The research and marketing of a product are very important parts of the design process, but you want to draw and design, right?

If you are in high school and think this field is where you want to be, Art Center and maybe other schools have Saturday classes for high school–level students. This can be a terrific way to get professional training early on, as well as a chance to work in the school's unique environment. It may be intimidating at first, but it can quickly become intoxicating, what with all the other projects and activities going on at the schools. It gives you insight to the comings and goings of the regular students and exposes you to lots of excellent student work. Unfortunately, this only works for the schools that provide this type of advanced high school training, and as I mentioned, Art Center is the only school I actually know that provides this.

Regardless of the level of your education, if you're still in school, it would be a good idea to take as many art classes as possible. Tell the instructor your particular interest in drawing or designing motorcycles, and ask if you can get some help and be allowed to pursue that goal. Most teachers are eager to help when a student has a specific objective and shows some initiative.

The addresses for the two institutions are:

Art Center College of Design
1700 Lida Street
Pasadena, CA 91103

College for Creative Studies
201 East Kirby
Detroit, MI 48202

Since its inception, the motorcycle has been an object of adventure, freedom, beauty, creativity, and fun. Many own one, and many more would like to have one. It is up to the future generations of chopper enthusiasts to continue the growth and interest that is being driven by today's creative and brilliant builders and designers.

Your job is to create that next imaginative, ingenious bike that looks cool, feels good, performs like no other, brings you huge returns, and sets the chopper world stampeding to you for everything you've got. Good luck.

# Appendix

Art Center College of Design
1700 Lida Street
Pasadena, CA 91103
www.artcenter.edu

Dave Bell
1834 Asbury Street
Falcon Heights, MN 55113

John Bell
www.johnbellstudio.com

Jim Bruni
Laguna Beach, California

College for Creative Studies
201 East Kirby
Detroit, MI 48202
www.ccscad.edu

Dave Deal
www.bigdealart.com

Bob Dron
Harley-Davidson of Oakland,
California
www.bobdron.com

Tom Fritz
www.fritzart.com

Darrell Mayabb
www.automotivegraffiti.com

Arlen Ness
www.arlenness.com

Charlie Smith
www.motorburg.com

Lance Sorchik
Sussex, New Jersey

Thom Taylor
www.hotrodthom@cox.net

Greg Tedder
www.58vw.com/tedder

Don Varner
don@onepasswaterblade.com

Keith Weesner
www.keithweesner.com

# Index

**How to Draw Cars Like a Pro**
ISBN 0-7603-0010-0

**How to Draw Cars the
Hot Wheels Way**
ISBN 0-7603-1480-2

**How to Draw Aircraft
Like A Pro**
ISBN: 0-7603-0960-4

**Choppers:
Heavy Metal Art**
ISBN 0-7603-2053-5

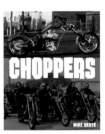

**Choppers**
ISBN 0-7603-1339-3

**Outlaw Choppers**
ISBN 0-7603-1849-2

**Techno-Chop**
ISBN 0-7603-2116-7

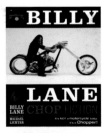

**Billy Lane:
Chop Fiction**
ISBN 0-7603-2011-X

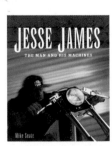

**Jesse James:
The Man and His Machines**
ISBN 0-7603-1614-7